P9-ARA-465

3 2711 00143 4079

DISCARD

DATE DUE

Nov 10 2009		
JAN 0 3 2010		
MAY 0 7 2012		

Demco, Inc. 38-293

Working with Cultural Differences

Recent Titles in
Contributions in Psychology

COLUMBIA COLLEGE LIBRARY
600 S. MICHIGAN AVENUE
CHICAGO, IL 60605

Working with Cultural Differences

Dealing Effectively with Diversity in the Workplace

RICHARD BRISLIN

Contributions in Psychology, Number 51
Paul Pedersen, Series Editor

Westport, Connecticut
London

Library of Congress Cataloging-in-Publication Data

Brislin, Richard W., 1945–
  Working with cultural differences : dealing effectively with diversity in the
workplace / Richard Brislin.
      p.   cm. — (Contributions in psychology, ISSN 0736–2714 ; no. 51)
    Includes bibliographical references and index.
    ISBN 978–0–313–35282–9 (alk. paper)
    1. Diversity in the workplace.   2. Interpersonal relations.   3. Intercultural
communication.   I. Title.
    HF5549.5.M5B74   2008
    658.3008—dc22   2008010126

British Library Cataloguing in Publication Data is available.

Copyright © 2008 by Richard Brislin

All rights reserved. No portion of this book may be
reproduced, by any process or technique, without the
express written consent of the publisher.

Library of Congress Catalog Card Number: 2008010126
ISBN: 978–0–313–35282–9
ISSN: 0736–2714

First published in 2008

Praeger Publishers, 88 Post Road West, Westport, CT 06881
An imprint of Greenwood Publishing Group, Inc.
www.praeger.com

Printed in the United States of America

The paper used in this book complies with the
Permanent Paper Standard issued by the National
Information Standards Organization (Z39.48–1984).

10 9 8 7 6 5 4 3 2 1

Contents

Series Foreword

Richard Brislin focuses the searchlight of psychological research on the ways that cultures—or multiculturalism—shape the workplace at the domestic and international levels. While the ideals of multicultural harmony have not always been achieved in the workplace, these ideals are an important part of the "American Experiment" in pluralistic democracy. That experiment has never been in greater danger and that danger relates directly to the global and domestic conflict between religions, cultures, and civilizations. In the necessary search for "homeland security," we are in danger of giving up the basic values of pluralism. Everywhere, from the dollar bill to the Statue of Liberty, we have articulated the ideals of multicultural harmony in what we say, but too often we depend on simplistic stereotypes in what we do.

This book builds upon critical incidents and multicultural experiences so that the readers can learn from their own mistakes and the mistakes of others. Experience is the best teacher ... but sometimes the cost of tuition is very high. Imagine the cost of every mistake made in a workplace that could have been avoided if the workers had been prepared. At the first level there is the cost of a failed project. At the next level there is the collateral damage to the organization and the many people involved in the project. At the third level there is the loss of opportunity cost. Finally, there is the emotional cost of failure that infects the organization and everyone attached to the project. The real cost of multicultural incompetence is huge, especially when compared to the relatively inexpensive ways that multicultural incompetence can be avoided through training.

A businessman going abroad on assignment was warned by a colleague to "watch out for the beentos." He received this information so often that he finally asked, "What is a beento?" He was told it was people who had "been to" this place or that place and now mistakenly considered themselves experts. This book is designed to help the sojourner avoid being labeled a "beento." The complexity of culture at the domestic and international level is acknowledged and the reader is guided in how best to manage that complexity in the workplace.

Each chapter adds a layer of understanding about (1) interacting; (2) adjusting; (3) patterns; (4) communicating; (5) managing conflict; (6) decision making; (7) gender issues; (8) power issues; (9) social norms; (10) workplace dynamics; (11) relationships; (12) psychological processes; and (13) final advice. These are practical suggestions that have been tried and that work outside the classroom. The data in these critical incidents combine and condense hundreds of successful careers in multicultural workplaces and provide a great variety of strategies for getting out of trouble when and if you make a mistake, as you most certainly will.

This book appears in the "Contributions in Psychology" series as one more example of how the field of applied psychology meets the needs of our rapidly changing society. Each book in this series has advanced our understanding of how psychology contributes to civilization, one small step at a time. This book provides a valuable lesson for those who question the importance of multicultural competences in the workplace. Although we know a great deal about the world around us, we know relatively little about ourselves, how we change, and how to facilitate that change process toward positive goals in the multicultural workplace.

Paul Pedersen
Professor Emeritus Syracuse University and Visiting Professor,
Department of Psychology, University of Hawaii
January 25, 2008

Acknowledgments

Some of the critical incidents developed from conversations with colleagues. I would like to thank D.P.S. Bhawuk, Julie Haiyan Chao, Qimei Chen, Geert Hofstede, Julia Nikulina Compton, Norman Feather, Gary Fontaine, Susan Hanggie, Kiyohiko Ito, Varaporn Jamklai, Lane Kelley, Eugene Kim, Laurel King, Shinobu Kitayama, Min-Sun Kim, Ben Kudo, Julie Lee, Karen Lee, Kwok Leung, Joyce Liu, Brent MacNab, Sharon Miyashiro, Cynthia Ning, Barbara Obermaier, Nicholas Ordway, Astrid Podsiadlowski, Kawpong Polyorat, Shakti Rana, Garr Reynolds, Robert Robinson, Michael Salzman, Keiko Shimazu, Lin Wen Shu, Helene Sokugawa, John Tang, Harry Triandis, Sheldon Varney, James Wills, Melinda Wood, Tomoko Yoshida, and Philip Zimbardo for their suggestions.

1

Introduction: Increasing Intercultural Interactions

INCREASING INTERCULTURAL CONTACT

Benjamin Franklin once said that there are two certainties in life: death and taxes. In today's complex and fast-moving world, we can add another. People will continue to come into extensive contact with individuals from other countries and other cultural backgrounds. There are many examples from many social arenas. Tourism is a growing industry, and businesspeople welcome visitors from other countries. Manufacturing is becoming an increasingly international set of ventures, and businesspeople accept overseas assignments in, and travel frequently to, other countries (Shenkar & Luo, 2008). One of my colleagues at the University of Hawaii business school rarely receives a suggestion when he asks the question, "Can anyone give me an example of products that you buy that are not international?" Few people can think of examples that are not international when aspects such as raw materials, component parts, production, shipping, marketing, and sales are considered. As more countries (e.g., Australia, Great Britain) see increases in the numbers of colleges students can attend, university administrators will welcome more international students from both developed and developing countries. All people involved in extensive international contact face challenges and must make adjustments. They will experience different work styles, different norms for meeting and talking with people, unfamiliar foods, challenges to their thinking about what is "right and proper," and differences in communication styles. In addition, they will have to make adjustments without the support of most of their friends and family members.

With this increasing number of long-term sojourns in other countries, people will eventually return home and will face an additional number of challenges summarized by the term "reverse culture shock." People's home countries do not remain static and they will change from the memories people hold of the weeks prior to their sojourn. People are often unprepared for the challenges of returning home (Vidal, Valle, Aragon, & Brewster, 2007), and this often makes the experience more stressful than the sojourn itself.

In addition to contract across national boundaries, there will also continue to be extensive interactions among culturally different people within any one nation. In the United States, for example, groups that used to be called "minority" are lobbying business and governments for more attention to their culturally influenced perspectives on work and social issues. They are demanding coursework in colleges and universities in which they are clearly represented and are not treated in a manner secondary to Anglo-Americans. At many colleges, students must take a course that introduces them to diversity concerns, and this course is part of their general education requirement that is necessary for graduation. Human resource specialists in organizations must be familiar with various laws and legal decisions that guarantee protections for aspects of diversity such as cultural and national background, gender, age, and sexual orientation. Fans of both college and professional sports cannot help but notice that virtually all teams have participants from a wide variety of national and cultural backgrounds. If coaches cannot work effectively with players from different backgrounds, they will find themselves without jobs. At times, the fact of cultural diversity in sports leads to humor. Question: "What is the fastest growing language in the National Football League?" Answer: Samoan.

Sports fans who follow professional basketball know that many stars in the National Basketball Association, not just everyday players, are from other countries. These include China, Germany, the Virgin Islands, France, Argentina, and Canada. I know schoolteachers who introduce geography by asking students about sportsstars and having the students point to a map indicating the country where they are from.

Are We Well-Prepared?

With the certainty of increasing intercultural contact, it is reasonable to ask the question, "Are we well-prepared?" Often, the answer is "no."

Many people grew up and were socialized in areas of the world where they interacted only with people very much like themselves. There was not anything that could be called ethnic or cultural diversity, and so people did not learn to interact in a respectful way to those who were different. Even if they did live in areas where culturally diverse individuals were present, social norms may have limited the types of interaction they could have. For example, they might frequently patronize the stores of culturally diverse people, but friendship formation would be a much rarer event. At times, these social norms involved labeling culturally diverse people in negative terms and involved denying them privileges reserved for preferred cultural groups.

In such cases, people are not only unprepared for effective intercultural interactions, but also, in addition to a lack of preparation, they may have to reverse and correct some of the cultural norms they learned during childhood. Many people face a dilemma. In years past, they learned to hold culturally diverse people at arms length. Today, they want those people as employers, customers, and in similar roles that require respectful interactions. There is some catching up to do.

The goal of this book is to introduce a wide range of concerns, and to present some practical advice, on ways of understanding and improving intercultural interactions.

Since many such interactions take place in the workplace and on international job assignments, the world of business will frequently be discussed. I believe that the points raised will often be applicable to understanding and improving intercultural contact in other arenas such as education, vacation travel, life in neighborhoods, and voluntary community activities. A term that will be frequently used is "sojourner." This is the term often used to describe people that spend a long period of time, approximately two years or more, in a culture other than the one in which they were socialized (Bochner, 2006). In addition, these people expect at some point to return to their own culture. The specification of two years is admittedly just an estimate. Many businesspeople who travel frequently to other countries may not spend two years in each, but their total collection of experiences is similar in intensity to people who accept an overseas assignment in one specific country. Another term sometimes used as a synonym for sojourner is "expatriate." I only use this term for people who do not intend to return to their own culture, for example, immigrants who cut all ties to their home countries.

ORGANIZATION OF THE BOOK

After this introductory Chapter 1, various aspects of international contact and intercultural interactions will be covered, always with many examples of actual challenges people have faced.

Chapter 2. Adjusting to Other Cultures. Moving from one's own culture, or facing the necessity of increased intercultural interactions within a large and complex country such as the United States, causes emotional upheavals. Topics include culture shock, adjusting to multiple role demands, and reverse culture shock upon returning to one's own culture (Kealey, 1989; 1996; Sussman, 2002).

Chapter 3. Individualism and Collectivism. Many specific cultural differences can be better understood if people are aware of broad concepts that can be used to describe cultures. One of the most helpful is individualism and collectivism. What is the emphasis within a culture? Is it the individual with her/his skills, attitudes, and personality; or is it the collective with the emphasis on group norms, cooperation, harmony, and doing one's duty within the group (Brewer & Chen, 2007; Markus & Kitayama, 1991; Triandis, 1995)?

Chapter 4. Communication: Interpreting Silence, Quiet, and Indirectness. Many communication difficulties during intercultural interactions arise because people misinterpret the meaning behind quietness, or silence, or a calm reaction where more enthusiasm was expected. Many times, there is "a storm behind the calm" about which people must be aware (Cushner & Brislin, 1996; Hall, 1959; Ikuko, 2006; Van de Vliert, 2007).

Chapter 5. Communication: Interpreting Directness and Potentially Negative Exchanges. In addition to interactions that are quiet and calm, other encounters involve more intense and negative emotions. Many times, the attributions about these incidents can become less negative if people understand the cultural basis for the intense reactions (Hammer, 1997).

Chapter 6. Dealing with Criticisms and Disagreements. In some cultures, public disagreements are rare events. Since people have little experience dealing with criticisms and disagreements, they are unprepared to interact in cultures where people feel that disagreements are healthy and beneficial since they bring various points of view out into the open. If they are not prepared for disagreements, many people interpret them as personal attacks (Jandt, 1998; Kaushal & Kwantes, 2006; Klyukanov, 2005; Ting-Toomey, 1985).

Chapter 7. Decision Making. People must gather information and make decisions among attractive alternatives. The ways in which decisions are made are influenced by people's culture, such as whether decisions are made in a public forum or in private. In addition, culture has an influence on the weights placed on various factors that enter the decision-making process (Chu, Spires, Farn, & Sueyoshi, 2005; Gupta & Govindarajan, 2000).

Chapter 8. Interactions among Males and Females. In some cultures, women have well-defined roles in the workplace, and they have difficulties entering the executive ranks. In other cultures, women have many leadership positions in business, government, and the professions. When women have had positions of power in a culture for several generations, it leads to an emphasis on quality of life issues such as government-sponsored health care, social services, and a balance between work and family life (Hofstede, 2001).

Chapter 9. Status and Power. All cultures give status to a select number of people, and to their decision-making power. Differences exist in the amount of status and deference high power people can expect, how easily power is shared and delegated (Littrell, 2007), and what behaviors are expected of high-status people. Americans often find more emphasis on status and power on overseas assignments than they expected (Osland & Bird, 2000).

Chapter 10. The Nature and Importance of Social Norms. People in all cultures want predictability on important issues such as ways of interacting successfully with others, professionalism in the workplace, and ways of planning for the future. When people develop agreed upon social norms, they increase the chances of predictable outcomes for themselves. Cultural differences exist concerning the targets of social norms, and the relative importance that people place on norms (Hofstede, 2001; House, Hanges, Javidan, Dorfman, & Gupta, 2004; Wan, Chiu, Peng, & Tam, 2007).

Chapter 11. Workplace Dynamics. Before accepting overseas assignments, or before assuming leadership positions in multicultural organizations, people have been successful in career-developing activities. They achieve their successes through the application of various workplace behaviors. In other cultures, these workplace behaviors have to be modified. Examples are organization of the workday, amount of formality and informality in the workplace, and expectations of late night socializing with coworkers (Dinsbach, Feij, & de Vries, 2007; Levine, 1997; Luo & Chen, 1996; Wang, Brislin, Wang, Williams, & Chao, 2000).

Chapter 12. Developing Interpersonal Relationships. Success in intercultural interactions is dependent on developing positive interpersonal relationships with colleagues and coworkers. The ways in which these relationships develop, the expectations of what "friendship" entails, and responses to favors offered to colleagues differ from culture to culture (Mak & Buckingham, 2007; Ross, 1977; Yoshida, 1994; Zimbardo & Lieppe, 1991).

Chapter 13. Basic Psychological Processes at Work during Intercultural Interactions. Life in other cultures does not entail an entirely different set of psychological principles that guide people's everyday lives. Rather, the same principles are at work with different emphases, different surface manifestations, and different behaviors to which the principles are applied. Examples include the need to categorize large amounts of information, responding appropriately to behaviors in different social contexts, and dealing with cultural differences and possibly misinterpreting unfamiliarity for prejudice (Aronson, Wilson, & Akert, 1999; Berry, Poortinga, & Pandey, 1997; Francesco & Gold, 1998; Herskovits, 1948).

Chapter 14. Some Final Pieces of Advice and Some Concluding Perspectives. Even though the challenges of extensive intercultural contact are formidable, they can be overcome if people understand the sources of cultural differences and understand a range of behavioral responses to deal with them. If they learn to identify and work well with individuals who have good advice to offer, such as cultural informants and professional interpreters, they will increase their chances of success. They can also reap the benefits of intercultural interactions such as broadened perspectives and more complex thinking about important social issues (Adler, 2002; Kagitcibasi, 1978).

USE OF CRITICAL INCIDENTS

Much of this book will consist of critical incidents and their explanations. Critical incidents for intercultural analyses are short stories that have characters, a theme, a plot line, and an ending that involves a puzzle or a misunderstanding. The purpose of critical incidents is to involve readers in the short stories and to have them empathize with the characters. Further, readers become involved and try to figure out what they would do if they were "in the shoes" of the characters (Cushner & Brislin, 1996; Thomas & Inkson, 2004). After presenting the incident, different concepts are introduced that explain the incident. Often, these explanations give the viewpoint of various people so that future sojourners can learn how their culture and the culture of others affect everyday workplace behaviors. Critical incidents start with a specific example, a story with characters and a plot, and later move to more general explanations that readers will hopefully find useful in interpreting many other incidents. This move from the specific to the general is preferable to the other direction of generalization followed by examples. With critical incidents, readers are immediately engaged because they want to know what happened to the people in the story. Once they read the story, they then are ready for more general explanations that have widespread applicability (Brislin & Yoshida, 1994).

Critical incidents have other advantages. They are the type of writing that comes closest to how people actually describe their intercultural experiences (e.g., Leung, 2007). People don't say, "I had an interesting challenge to my thinking about attributional processes," even though attributions are discussed in Chapter 13. People are much more likely to describe a specific encounter with individuals from another culture and to report how puzzling or amusing or memorable it was. I hope in this book that people can move from an understanding of specific incidents to an understanding of concepts that will be helpful in interpreting many different intercultural encounters. Hopefully, some of these incidents that will be more fully understood will be similar to the experiences people will actually have as sojourners.

2

Adjusting to Other Cultures

DIFFERENT PATTERNS OF ADJUSTMENT
TO OTHER CULTURES

When people from two different cultures come together and interact, they have choices concerning their behaviors (Kealey, 1989, 1996; Shute, 2007; Sussman, 2002). Consider the example of a businessman from China and a businesswoman from the United States. During negotiations in preparation for a possible joint venture, they can negotiate in a style familiar in China or familiar in the United States. Where do the negotiations take place? This is a key factor, because there is often a "home court advantage" in intercultural interactions, with negotiations proceeding according to the norms of the culture where the interactions are taking place.

However, taking advantage of the home court advantage is not always the best option. At times, it is wiser to take into account the preferences of one's negotiating partner so that interactions will proceed more smoothly. This is especially true when the negotiating partners have not been involved in international ventures and have not had much experience dealing with businesspeople from other countries. If people are aware of behaviors that are familiar in both cultures, there are four general patterns of choices they can make when interacting with individuals from the other culture. The four patterns (adapted from Berry & Sam, 1997) are based on answers to two questions: Do people want to behave according to norms that are familiar in their own culture? Do people want to behave according to norms that are familiar in the other culture? Since we are considering the preferences of people from two cultures (culture A and B), there are four combinations of yes-no answers. In this example, interactions are taking place in culture A. People from culture B will be referred to by the common term "sojourners," or people interacting in a culture other than their own. People from culture A will be referred to as the "hosts."

	Do people in Culture B (sojourners) want to behave according to their familiar norms?	
Do people in Culture A (hosts) want to behave according to their familiar norms?	yes	no
yes	People integrate their preferences	People accommodate to preferences in culture B
no	People assimilate to the preferences of Culture A and their "home court advantage"	People reject the preferences of both culture, risking confusion and ineffectiveness

When people from both cultures are aware of preferences and differences and try to take them into account, they try to integrate their efforts. This pattern is typical of individuals who know about and respect cultural differences. Assisting people who want to work according to this pattern is a major goal of this book.

When hosts insist that sojourners behave according to the norms of culture A, people from culture B must either assimilate to these demands or cease interactions. This pattern, where people impose their home court advantage, is far more common than might be expected at first glance. When hosts do not know much about culture and cultural differences, they may not realize that they are imposing themselves when they expect sojourners to behave according to culture A's norms. This pattern of assimilation is often based on ignorance.

When hosts are willing to interact according to the norms familiar to people in culture B, they are engaging in accommodation. Hosts set aside their own preferences and encourage sojourners to interact in ways that they bring from their culture B. This can be a very effective way to behave as long as hosts are very knowledgeable about culturally different interaction styles. In my experience, there are *individuals* who can behave effectively in this manner. But there are rarely large number of people within any one host-country organization who can successfully accommodate to the preferences of sojourners.

If all people set aside their preferences, perhaps out of a misguided attempt to find an undefined common ground, confusion and chaos may result. People need firm anchoring in a set of norms for effective interpersonal interactions. These can come from one's own culture or from knowledge about and sensitivity to another culture. Without such an anchoring, ineffective interactions are a certainty.

Emotional Ups and Downs during Adjustment

The pattern of adjustment I recommend, known as integration, involves respect both for one's own cultural background and the different backgrounds of other people from other countries. Even when accepting this pattern, however, people experience emotional challenges as they try to implement their goal of cultural sensitivity and respect for others (Bochner, 1994; Shute, 2007; Sussman, 2002; Takeuchi, Lepak, Marinova, &Yun, 2007). Take the example of an American businesswoman on a two-year assignment in Japan. Upon arrival in Tokyo, there is often a honeymoon phase because there are so many new experiences, new sights, new foods to try, the challenge of an overseas job, and so forth. Many times, the honeymoon phase results from overly optimistic assumptions about the ease of cultural adjustment. When this optimism is challenged by the problems that every sojourner eventually faces (Adler, 2003), the businesswoman is likely to have a mood-swing that moves her toward much more negativism in her everyday thinking.

Disappointments during the honeymoon phase add up to a reaction called "disillusion." No one disappointment would cause disillusion and negative emotions, but the experiences surrounding many adjustment difficulties add up quickly. In Japan, the businesswoman will find it difficult to find affordable housing. She will have to master a new public transportation system whose subway cars can become extremely crowded during rush hours. She will have to adjust to a new workplace with a different set of norms for everyday behavior. She may have to work with bosses and colleagues who are unfamiliar with women who have high level positions in their companies. She will miss familiar foods and the company of old friends with whom she could share her trials and tribulations. If she is married, she needs to be concerned about the needs of her husband and whether or not he has meaningful activities. If she was offered a position in Japan but he was not, he has the status of a "trailing spouse" who will begin a job search after arrival in Tokyo. If he has difficulties, these will have an impact on the marriage.

Most people overcome the disillusion stage and begin to accommodate to their new culture. They often are helped by sympathetic hosts who themselves have had an overseas experience. As people learn more about the host culture and modify their original over-optimistic expectations based on multiple reality checks, they enter a stage called "satisfaction." They become much more effective in their day-to-day management of life's demands such as transportation, food, and after-work social activities. They learn acceptable norms for everyday interactions with colleagues and bosses in the workplace. Their spouses find acceptable positions. While rarely matching the enthusiasm of their honeymoon period, this period of satisfaction allows people to be effective in the workplace and to enjoy their sojourns.

The language of adjustment is borrowed from the experiences of newlyweds. Parents tell their children that the honeymoon will hopefully be great, but after this period they will have to settle into the hard work of making a marriage successful.

The need to make many adjustments in a short period of time is the theme of this incident.

So Many Adjustments, So Little Time

Beth Foley worked in New York City for an international bank that had branch offices in many of the world's large cities. One day, her supervisor offered her a major position at the office in Seoul, Korea. Beth discussed the possible move with her husband. They also talked to their older two children, ages eleven and eight, who were reminded that they might have to spend more time looking after their two-year-old sister. Family members agreed that it would be a good career move for Beth and so she reported her positive decision to her supervisor. Beth's husband knew he would be a "trailing spouse." Given his expertise in computer technology, he hoped to land a job once the family arrived in Seoul.

After arriving in Seoul, Beth faced multiple demands on her time. She met and interacted with coworkers. She spoke with various Korean supervisors to whom she would report. With her husband, she sought housing, schools for the older two children, and day care for the youngest. After the excitement of the first few weeks, Beth became irritable and unenthusiastic about the position in Seoul. Coworkers noted that she was not very productive, and relations with her husband and children became strained at home.

Beth may be experiencing culture shock. Many people who live for extensive periods of time in another culture experience symptoms such as: an irritable mood, difficulty sleeping, loss of appetite, upset stomach, headaches, and decreased enthusiasm about life in general. One reason for culture shock is that the familiar methods of achieving everyday goals are suddenly taken away. For example, Beth has to meet and interact with colleagues and supervisors, but she has to do this in culturally appropriate ways in Korea. Familiar workplace behaviors learned in her own culture may no longer be suitable and in some cases may be totally inappropriate.

Another reason for culture shock is that so many adjustments have to be made in a very short period of time. The sense of "feeling overwhelmed" is common (Brislin, 2000). In this example, Beth faces workplace challenges but also must find schools and day care for the children, must figure out Seoul's transportation system, must support her husband in his job search, and so forth.

Programs that prepare people for overseas assignments often cover culture shock reactions. Moving people away from the feelings that "I am the only one with these problems" can hasten their adjustment and job effectiveness.

Often, reasons for culture shock and adjustment problems occur because difficulties were unexpected and people never took the time to prepare themselves for potential problems.

Unexpected Stress on Overseas Assignments

Heather Martin and Michelle Collins had been apartment mates during their four years of college study. They were both business administration majors and had taken courses that would provide good preparation for an overseas assignment. They found that they had similar interests in music, computer technology, and athletics. They even dated the same man at different times and broke up with him for similar reasons.

After graduation, Heather took a position in Bangkok, Thailand, and Michelle agreed to join a company in Brisbane, Australia. They kept in frequent e-mail and telephone contact during their assignments and they shared their reactions to life in another country. They were surprised to find that Michelle had a more difficult adjustment to Australia compared to Heather's experiences in Thailand.

People often have a difficult time adjusting to a culture that is "supposedly similar." In Michelle's case, there is a shared language, some similarities given many citizens' European roots, and the possibility of shared interests such as boating and hiking.

But there are also identifiable reasons for potential difficulties. One is that given an assumed similarity, people are not prepared to experience differences. When the cultural differences do appear, they have a large impact given people's lack of preparation. Another reason is that given the shared language, people can form relationships quicker. But relationships, whether they are based on romances, friendships, or frequent workplace interactions, sometimes go sour and this causes stress among the people concerned.

A third reason is that people may not be given "much slack." If an American makes a cultural mistake in Thailand, it may be overlooked as long as she shows a desire to be culturally sensitive. Similar mistakes may be much more noticeable in Australia if the assumption is that "Americans should know this and should know the proper way of doing things." For example, Australians often ridicule Americans who call too much attention to themselves: "tall poppies" are taken down a peg (Mandisodza, Jost, & Unzueta, 2006).

People can receive cross-cultural training (Brislin & Yoshida, 1994; Sanchez-Burks, Lee, Nisbett, &Ybarra, 2007; Singelis, 1998) to prepare them for adjustment difficulties, but it is important to offer the training at the most appropriate time. In Michelle's case, she simply might dismiss information about possible problems while still in the United States. A better time to discuss difficulties may be a few weeks into her assignment in Australia. At this point, she is likely to have experienced some cultural differences and will be more willing to take them seriously.

Multiple Small Adjustments

Another reason for the stress of culture shock is that people have to make many small adjustments in a short period of time. Each adjustment causes a little bit of difficulty, but the stress adds up to a point where people become frustrated and begin to complain about their life in the other culture. This process of small stresses adding up can be seen in this incident involving an Australian woman living in Boston. As in the previous incident, the culture shock is exacerbated because few or no cultural differences were expected given that people thought they would be using the same language.

Dealing with Many Small Differences Can Cause Exhaustion

"It's not that I want to return to Australia, it's just that I feel exhausted here in America." Fiona Elliot was sharing her experiences in an e-mail to an old high school friend in Brisbane, Queensland. Fiona had graduated from the University of Sydney with an advanced degree in biology. Seeking to expand her work experience, she accepted a job with a biotechnology firm in Boston, Massachusetts. She hoped to become involved in the development of improved drugs for adult onset diabetes.

Given that her native language was English, Fiona expected few adjustment difficulties to life in the United States. However, she found herself dealing with a number of small frustrations. People in Boston found her Australian accent difficult to understand and seemed to put no effort into listening more carefully. She discovered that she knew more about current events in America than any five people knew about events in Australia.

She tried to keep up with world events by watching American television shows with the title, "International News." However, she felt these television shows covered a small number of news stories and did so from an American perspective.

She found that similar activities have very different connotations. She would go to a pub to have a beer and to chat with people. In Boston, she learned that men and women don't simply socialize in a pleasant manner. In sharp contrast to Australia, bars in America are "meet markets" where people have goals other than pleasant conversation. She would try to be humorous in a droll, sometimes sarcastic manner that she learned in Australia. But instead of finding humor in her statements, Americans would become attentive and say, "Oh, really!" She became frustrated making so many choices when she shopped. She commented that she had to expend energy choosing among breakfast cereals, types of bread when she ordered a sandwich, and how she wanted her coffee beans ground.

No one of the experiences reported by Fiona should cause difficulties adjusting to life in the United States. However, these reactions to many experiences add up over time and can lead to feelings of exhaustion. People from other English-speaking countries are sometimes invited to workshops on cross-cultural adjustment shortly after their arrival in the United States. They often turn these invitations down, arguing that they don't expect any problems. Only later do they learn the lesson, "Dealing with many small unexpected difficulties can lead to adjustment challenges."

The process of adjustment to another culture is aided if people have a good sense of humor. Difficulties are inevitable, but if people keep smiling and tell themselves that what is happening will make for amusing stories someday, then adjustment will be hastened.

Looking for a Sense of Humor

"We need to find the best person possible for this overseas assignment," Diane Kim said to Bert O'Brien. Diane was the president of an office equipment company in Sacramento and Bert was the personnel director. They wanted to hire a marketing director who would be based in Paris. They decided to advertise widely in publications such as the *Wall Street Journal* and the *New York Times*. In addition to sales experience, Diane insisted that the qualifications called for a sense of humor. Bert reminded her that this would make the announcement more expensive, since the publications charged by the word. Diane replied that it would be a good use of funds.

Having a sense of humor facilitates overseas assignments. Working overseas inevitably bring stress given that people have to make multiple adjustments to differences in work styles, relations with both superiors and subordinates, interactions with customers, and many other job and personal issues. Further, they often have to struggle in a second language.

If people respond to frustrations by becoming upset and irritated, they experience a set of reactions that can threaten their health. Their blood pressure can rise, they can experience nausea, they may have difficulties eating and sleeping, and they can develop tension headaches. But if people can laugh and joke about their difficulties, these potentially damaging physiological reactions do not occur.

Seeing the humor in frustrating situations involves more active thinking than becoming stressed out. Humor stems from understanding two or more categories that do not normally occur together and finding the "twist" that unites them. The discovery of the twist leads to the pleasurable experiences of smiling and laughing. A musician tells friends, "I thought 'Smoke gets in your eyes' was a song until I went to Los Angeles, where it was a weather report." Two categories, a lounge singer's standard and air quality, are being combined, and seeing the quirky reason for the combination is the basis of the humor. If people on overseas assignments think in this active manner during their humorous observations, they may also think about various ways of dealing with problems that they encounter.

Another advantage of using humor is that it signals to others that a person is pleasant and approachable. If a person is glum and complaining, others may keep their distance. But if a person can laugh and make jokes, others may come forward to offer various kinds of social support (Glazer, 2006).

Often, people find that they make adjustments to another culture gradually (Bhasar-Shrinivas, Harrison, Shaffer, & Luk, 2005), over a period of six months to a year. Given that the changes are gradual, they may not notice that their behavior is quite different in the other culture compared to behavior in their own culture. It is their friends who, seeing them for the first time in a year, say, "You've changed so much!"

Fitting into Group Norms

Janet Fujimoto, originally from Los Angeles, worked in Honolulu for a large Japanese-owned hotel chain. She was well-known to executives in Hawaii as a "fast tracker." This reputation was aided by her outgoing personality and willingness to take on projects beyond her job description. She was offered an assignment at company headquarters in Tokyo and accepted the position with enthusiasm.

Over the first six months of her assignment in Tokyo, Janet sensed changes in her behavior. She found herself dressing in a more conservative manner and wearing less makeup. She was careful not to disagree in public with her older male supervisors. If she had the opportunity to work on projects outside her written job responsibilities, she made sure that she did not encroach on a coworker's efforts. Even though she might want to spend time on her own interests and hobbies outside of work, she was careful to accept social invitations offered by coworkers.

Janet is adjusting to Japanese expectations that she fit into a group rather than stand out as a unique individual. Norms refer to shared and agreed-upon behaviors, and they guide people in a wide variety of social interactions. The Japanese workplace has many social norms, and people are expected to pay careful attention to them. One of the most important norms is that people should not call too much attention to themselves. They should "fit in" and they signal acceptability of this norm with their dress, interactions with older supervisors, and cooperative efforts with coworkers. As children, all Japanese learn the adage, "The nail that sticks up gets hammered down." In the workplace, they frequently use this saying when observing someone who behaves differently from same-age peers. Norms help people deal with an uncertain future. We may not know exactly what will happen in ten years. But if norms are taken seriously, we have the comfort of knowing that today's standards of behavior will still be in effect.

People frequently ask the question, "Are these norms changing?" The answer is, "Not fast enough for the most ambitious and career-oriented Japanese women." Good advice for people assigned to Japan is to seek out coworkers who can answer questions about the importance of certain norms, the amount of deviation allowed, and whether or not the norms seem to be changing.

Reentering One's Own Culture

People often experience another type of culture shock when they return home. If they have been overseas for two years, time had not stood still in their communities! As with many aspects of adjustment, reverse culture shock is intensified if people are unprepared for its impact (Brislin & Yoshida, 1994).

Returning Home from an International Assignment

"I've learned a lot on this overseas assignment, but it will be good to get home," Bill Evans thought to himself during the going-away party his colleagues arranged for him. Bill had been working at the Hong Kong branch of a large investment firm for three years, and he was about to return to the Chicago home office. He was looking forward to seeing old associates at work, and he even planned to look up his former girlfriend.

After an enthusiastic welcome back at the Chicago office, Bill began to feel a sense of discontent. His stories of life in Hong Kong were met with blank stares. He found that his work assignments dealing with domestic issues in the United States were uninteresting and seemingly unimportant. His old girlfriend was seeing someone else. He began to feel that his three years in Hong Kong was not the career advancer that his old boss said it would be.

Bill may be experiencing reverse culture shock. Many people who accept overseas assignments go through a period of stress known as culture shock as they adjust to new demands in another country. These same people often experience reverse culture shock upon their return home (Vidal et al., 2007). Reverse culture shock can often be extremely intense, since people don't expect difficulties. People often think, "What can be easier than returning to my home and to the country I know so well?"

Reasons for reverse culture shock include the reactions of others. Old colleagues have difficulties relating to the stories that returnees tell since they have not had similar experiences. "People listen to my stories for about fifteen minutes, but at minute number sixteen they start looking at their watches," returnees complain. People who were subordinates in the workplace may have been promoted and so the returnees have a new boss and must develop a different type of relationship. Old friends are likely to have experienced various life changes, which give them less time for interactions with returnees. The line from the old song, "Wedding bells have broken up that old gang of mine," becomes applicable.

Personnel specialists in an organization's human resources division can offer programs to prepare people for reverse culture shock, but attendance at such programs can be disappointingly small. People rarely consider the possibility of reverse culture shock and find the thought of attending a special program on "returning home" as a strange use of their time.

LONG-TERM IMPACTS OF SOJOURNS

Even with their adjustment difficulties and their experiences with reverse culture shock (Bolino, 2007), most people view their overseas experiences as extremely important in their lives. After readjusting, they often find themselves in the company of others who have had overseas experiences, even if the experiences have not been in the same country. This important result of extensive intercultural interactions is sometimes referred to as "participating in a third culture."

Sharing a Third Culture

Sven Janssen and Gail Ogawa found themselves chatting with each other after Chamber of Commerce meetings in Burlington, Vermont. Sven worked for a frozen foods manufacturer and Gail worked for a bank.

Both were romantically involved with other people. They first started talking with each other after a meeting where international business for Vermont's future was discussed.

Both Sven and Gail contributed to the discussion. They approached each other and at the same time asked, "You've lived overseas, haven't you?" Sven said that he had, being the son of Swedish missionaries, and had spent time in several countries, including Ghana. Gail had been the daughter of military personnel and had lived in several countries where the United States had Army bases. Her high school years were spent in Germany. After a few months during which they spent time together, people who knew both Sven and Gail could not figure out what they had in common. Friends would comment, "They have totally different personalities and don't have any shared hobbies or interests that we can see."

Sven and Gail share what is called a "third culture" (Gaw, 2007; Pollock & Van Reken, 1999). It is not the culture where they were born or the culture where they are currently living. Rather, it is a third place that demanded that they adjust to different expectations about everyday behaviors, learn another language, attend schools with different philosophies of education, and so forth. This third culture does not have to be the same place. Sven and Gail may not have lived in the same country. What they now share are international experiences and adjustments to cultural differences in places where their parents had previously lived.

Another implication of third culture experiences is that people learn to set their own goals and work toward them. For example, if they are to make friends, they have to figure out ways of doing this in different cultures. Few junior high-school students anywhere in the world come up to newcomers and say, "Welcome to our school! Can I introduce you to others?" Rather, the third culture newcomers must make efforts to meet others, form friendships, and to balance schoolwork with social activities. This leads to a "can do" attitude useful in later career development.

SOME FINAL COMMENTS: SUCCESS IN INTERCULTURAL INTERACTIONS

Acknowledgment of cultural differences, and of the dynamics of intercultural interactions, contributes to success on overseas assignments. When "success" is discussed, people are expected to satisfy four criteria.

The first aspect of the "criteria for success" is that sojourners enjoy their intercultural assignments, feel that they are making positive contributions to their organization, and report good working relationships with others. The second aspect is that these other people, from different cultural backgrounds, reciprocate these positive feelings. This requirement that positive feelings about work, contributions, and relationships be shared protects us against certain rigid and overconfident people. These people may report good working relationships, but if others are interviewed they might disagree and share their feelings that the sojourners should have stayed home.

The third aspect is that people complete tasks in a timely and effective manner. Overseas business people should be able to complete negotiations for joint trade agreements, international students should complete their degree studies, and technical assistance advisors should be able to introduce various technologies. The fourth aspect is that people manage the unique stresses associated with overseas assignments. These unique stresses are referred to as "culture shock," and they result from the necessity of accomplishing tasks in unfamiliar ways. Familiar cultural practices are often not effective in other countries and sojourners must learn new ways of accomplishing their goals. Further, they must engage in this new learning without their helpful and familiar support group from their own country.

The four aspects of intercultural success are strongly related. If sojourners have good relationships with coworkers in other countries, this can contribute to task completion. Good relationships can lead to a support group that can assist sojourners through the stresses of culture shock. If sojourners are aware that cultural differences have an impact on their job performance, they can ask members of their newly developed support group for help in understanding the differences.

3

Individualism and Collectivism

THE SELF AND THE GROUP

Intercultural adjustment can be hastened if people know what to expect, and much of this book suggests applications of research on cultural differences that sojourners are likely to encounter. Some of the most helpful advice comes from research on individualism and collectivism (Brewer & Chen, 2007; Gudykunst, 1998; Hofstede, 2001; Markus & Kitayama, 1998; Triandis, 1995). A major source of cultural differences stems from people's concern with themselves as individuals and with themselves as members of groups. People all around the world have both concerns, but cultural guidelines put different emphases on individual and group concerns. We can start with the question, "What is the basic unit of society?" In an individualistic country such as the United States, the answer reflects concern with unique people and their freedoms, their attitudes, their life goals, and so forth. Certainly people come together for activities that demand group effort, such as the formation of nuclear families, but the cultural emphasis is on individuals and what they want to do with their lives.

In a collectivist culture, the answer to the question is that the basis unit is groups of people. Often, the group is an extended family, and it can also be one's organization in which a person has traditionally expected lifetime employment. The concerns of groups take precedence over the concerns of individuals. People are expected to sacrifice for the good of their groups.

The difference can be captured by looking at an aspect of work with which many readers are familiar: work outside the home as teenagers. In individualist nations, many teenagers earn their own spending money with part-time jobs. Examples are babysitting, lawn work, newspaper delivery, and jobs in fast food restaurants. Parents often encourage such work, feeling that it is good for teenagers to earn their own money. Individualist teenagers can also exercise their personal initiative and entrepreneurial spirit with such work. Part-time jobs also contribute to a unique sense of personal identity: "I am different from others with my combination of intramural basketball, math club membership, and weekend work mowing lawns or shoveling snow."

In collectivist nations, there is not an emphasis of developing a unique identity that would be aided by part-time work. In addition, the major focus of people's attention is their families. If teenagers have some extra time, there is surely someone in the extended family who can use an extra hand with daily tasks or occasional needs such as building an extension to a home. In collectivist nations, teenagers also are expected to follow well-established norms. These often include good performance in school, and so extra time is more likely to be spent on homework than on part-time wage-earning work.

The Sense of Self. There are four features of individualism and collectivism that summarize many of the reasons for cultural differences (Bhawuk, 2001; Triandis, 1995).

The first is the sense of a person's self. With individualists, the self consists of thoughts that involve "I" or "me." When asked to describe themselves, individualists are more likely to use sentences that focus on their unique features, such as "I am hard working," or "I am dedicated to country music." Collectivists are far more likely to have thoughts that focus on "we." When asked to describe themselves, they are far more likely to indicate their membership in groups with words like "son," "godparent," or "employee of the Sony corporation." When responding to multiple pieces of information in their environments, individualists are more likely to focus on what will affect them as unique people. Collectivists are more likely to focus on what will affect their extended family, religious ties, relations with others, or company where they work.

Goals to Pursue. A second feature distinguishing individualistic from collectivist nations centers on the pursuit of goals. People in individualistic countries are more likely to set their own personal goals and to work toward their accomplishment. One of the clearest examples is marriage. People want a happy marriage, and they seek this out by choosing a mate. There may be comments made by family members about the choice, but the decision is ultimately up to the individual. In a collectivist culture, people are more likely to integrate the goals of others in the formation of their own goals. Before he came to the United States for the goal of advanced study, my friend from collective Nepal had to integrate the wishes of others. He had to consult his uncles for their approval. He had to make sure his parents would be looked after. After he became settled in the United States, he knew that he would have to sponsor and financially support other family members who wanted to leave Nepal. His marriage was arranged. He deferred to the wisdom of his fathers and uncles who selected a wife for him. He did not meet his wife until the day of the marriage. The focus of marriage in a collectivist culture is not the two individuals most clearly involved. The focus is a relationship between two extended families, and what the implications of the marriage will be for all family members.

Attitudes and Norms. The third feature distinguishing individualist and collectivist nations is the relative emphasis on attitudes and norms. In individualist cultures, the focus is on unique people and their unique perspectives. Consequently, there is great emphasis placed on people's attitudes, beliefs, and opinions. The entire public opinion polling industry is based on people's willingness to answer questions about their attitudes and beliefs. When making decisions concerning where to live and work, people refer to their attitudes about various factors such as the area's climate, leisure time activities, opportunities for promotion in the workplace, and so forth.

In collectivist cultures, there is more emphasis on norms considered important in people's groups. Norms refer to standards of behavior that group members are expected to follow. People refer to these norms in making decisions about their behavior, and they often behave in certain ways "because they are supposed to." In cultures where strong kinship obligations are normative, people get along with their cousins because that is what is expected. There are far fewer decisions based on attitudes about specific cousins, for example, that one cousin is liked more than others. The norm is to interact smoothly with cousins, and so that is what people do. In making decisions about where to live and work, people in collectivist nations are more likely to be attentive to norms. People will stay near the homes of their parents because they are expected to take care of them in their old age.

They will set aside preferences for their own career paths (e.g., teaching, dentistry) if they are expected to accept a responsible position in their families' businesses.

Rational and Relational Interactions. The fourth distinction deals with people's interactions with others. Individualists often have a few close friends and close ties with their nuclear families, but interactions with people outside this close circle are known as "rational." This means that people keep up relations with others as long as there is usefulness in doing so. When the interactions are no longer useful, people cease their communication with these "others." The term "network" is common in individualist culture. Network members trade favors, and people remain in a network relationship as long as they continue to receive benefits. They can drop people from network membership if favors are not returned. People keep up contact with old high school and college friends if there is a good reason given their current career goals.

People in a collectivist nation are more likely to have a relational orientation. Once interactions with others become frequent and pleasant, people are likely to treat the others as if they belong to the same collective. There is not as much checking on "what favors have been offered and what favors have been returned?" People have a good relationship, and that should be the basis of people's decisions about their behavior. Compared to colleagues in individualist nations, I receive far more Christmas cards and "I'm just staying in touch" e-mails from people in collectivist counties with whom I worked with twenty years ago. According to the relational orientation, people have successful interactions, begin to feel as if they are in each other's collectives, and so will be interacting for many years to come.

THE MOVEMENT BETWEEN INDIVIDUALISTIC AND COLLECTIVISTIC CULTURES

Tensions arise when cultures come into contact, for instance, individualist (living in a collectivist culture) pursuing their own goals and not taking those of their group into account. Several critical incidents deal with issues faced by individualists living in collectivist cultures, and by collectivists living in individualistic cultures. At times, people can be humorous about cultural clashes, as in this example.

Arranging Job Interviews: Whose Responsibility?

Ramon Garcia, from a medium-sized city in Mexico, was attending the University of Arizona on a tennis scholarship. He had won an award for excellence in the classroom and on the tennis court. His graduation date was to be May 19, and in late April he found himself in odd social situations. He would see friends on campus and they would ask, "How are you?" followed by, "How are the job interviews going?" He mentioned to a professor, "I can respond to the first question but am stuck for an answer to the second."

One possible reason for Ramon's dilemma is that he is from a collectivist culture. In such cultures, people's identify is closely related to their membership in various social groups. As a result, people learn to think of themselves in terms of their relationships with others, their social obligations, and social norms they are expected to uphold. In contrast, people from individualist cultures, such as the United States, place more emphasis on unique aspects of themselves when they consider their identities. This means that there will be more emphasis on their skills, attitudes, opinions, and personal goals.

There are certainly exceptions, such as very group-oriented and sociable people who live in individualist cultures. Still, the distinction between individualism and collectivism helps suggest reasons for difficulties such as the one experienced by Ramon. In an individualist culture, who has the responsibility for setting up a good set of job interviews? The answer is "the person, himself or herself." Consequently, when graduating seniors greet each other on campus, a question about the job interview process makes sense.

Who has the responsibility for job interviews in a collectivist culture? The answer might be "the person's family and other members of important groups." In Ramon's case, his father, uncles, and cousins could have the responsibility of finding jobs or job interviews for him. He will follow through with the interviews after he returns to Mexico. Ramon is benefiting from his membership in a collectivist culture. However, he cannot expect to always be the recipient of favors and special treatment. Once he is well-established in a career, he will be obliged to provide various opportunities for relatives and long-time family friends.

Individualism and collectivism are important concepts that should be understood rather than judged as "better or worse." In Hawaii, many people have strong collective ties. Leaders and managers are well advised to know about their employees' family obligations and membership in long-term networks in addition to their individual skills and talents.

People from individualistic cultures will find that job interviews in collectivist culture may proceed in ways that are unfamiliar to them.

The Job Search: Meeting Interviewer Expectations

Jane McNeal, originally from Dallas, had worked for two years as an English Language teacher in Osaka. She had applied for teaching positions in Japan after graduating from college. She was now applying for positions in private sector corporations in Japan and recently completed her first job interview. One of the Japanese interviewers asked her about activities in college beyond her coursework. Jane replied that she had participated in many activities during her college years: as a member of an intramural volleyball team, two years with the college newspaper, one year as an officer in an academic honor society, and volunteer community work at the Blood Bank. The Japanese interviewers seemed puzzled with Jane's response to the question, and she had the feeling that the interview had not gone well.

A complex event such as a job interview will be affected by people's cultural backgrounds, personalities, past work experiences, amount of preparation, and other factors. One set of insights into Jane's feelings about a poor interview is based on cultural differences. Japan is a collectivist culture, and long-term loyalty to a group and the ability to work well with other group members are highly valued. The United States is an individualistic nation and people are expected to present skills, abilities, and positive work attitudes when they enter the job market.

Activities during college years are valued in both collectivistic and individualistic nations, but the reasons for the activities are different. In Japan, college students often join one group as freshmen and are very active in that group through their senior year. With these experiences, they are demonstrating their ability to develop and maintain long-term group commitments. In the United States, students often join several groups to develop various skills and to demonstrate that they are well-rounded. They also show their individualism with unique combinations of clubs and volunteer work, as in the example of Jane's varied activities.

There are various benefits that stem from successful membership in a collectivist or individualist culture. With collectivism, people have access to well-developed support groups that they can call upon when faced with various life challenges. However, they may face disapproval if they have ambitions to rise above the level of people who are similar in age and educational level. With individualism, people can pursue their own goals and can rise to high organizational levels based on their demonstrated skills and accomplishments. However, they do not necessarily have access to a strong support group that can assist them in dealing with stresses in their work and personal lives.

CHALLENGES TO FEELINGS ABOUT ETHICS AND TRUST

People from individualistic cultures will almost certainly encounter challenges to their sense of right and wrong when living in other cultures. Many such challenges stem from the collectivist demands that people must be loyal to group members. Individualists need to understand the pressures that will be put on collectivists if they do not fulfill the cultural expectations surrounding group loyalty.

Hiring Relatives: Nepotism or Group Loyalty?

"Sixteen thousand feet last weekend," John Reardon told Vishnu Sharma during a shared coffee break. John and Vishnu worked for an engineering firm in Kathmandu, Nepal, and John was referring to the altitude he had reached on his last mountaineering venture. After more talk about recent weekend activities, John mentioned that a new manager had been hired. He told Vishnu that the new hire was the nephew of the company vice president, and that several highly qualified university graduates had been passed over. John said, "Where I come from, British Columbia in Canada, such a hire would be a problem and the vice president would be accused of nepotism." Vishnu said, "I know all this, and in fact I was on the hiring committee that recommended the nephew."

John and Vishnu are bringing different cultural perspectives to this discussion. John comes from an individualistic culture where the emphasis is on the person and his or her skills, abilities, and potential contributions to the workplace. "Family connections" are less important, and there are often laws that prohibit hirings based on family relationships. Cultural values (Smith & Schwartz, 1997) include the strong possibility of overcoming a modest family background if people are willing to work hard and to develop skills attractive to the job market.

Nepal is a collectivist country where group norms, family obligations, and long-term loyalties are valued. The nephew is considered an acceptable hire because, in the ideal case, he will be loyal to the company and will work hard to please his influential uncle. Even if his qualifications are inadequate today, these can be upgraded with mentoring and training programs. Executives will view these activities as good long-term investments since the nephew will stay with the company for his entire career.

I work with people who are from collectivist nations such as Nepal, Japan, China, and India. They suggest that people consider what will happen if the uncle supports another candidate. Who can call on the phone or barge into the uncle's home to voice complaints? Will older family members make comments such as, "The great company vice president won't help his nephew! Isn't he forgetting that we took care of his wife and children while he was studying for his master's degree in the United States?" Not all cultural differences are easy and comfortable to analyze, but if people can put themselves in others' shoes, the reasons for culturally influenced behaviors will become clearer.

Understanding individualism and collectivism is important in the development of business relationships, especially when trust (Simpson, 2007) has to be part of joint venture agreements among companies.

Trust Can Take a Long Time to Develop

"Let's compare notes on our trips," Susan Nolan suggested to two of her colleagues. Susan, Mike James, and Judy Barth worked for an office supplies company in Atlanta, Georgia. The company both imported products that were manufactured abroad and also sought various international markets for direct sales to various businesses. The three division managers had recently traveled to Venezuela, Indonesia, and Spain. The three agreed that, after meeting potential collaborators and clients in these three countries, it took a long time to "get down to business."

They shared other common experiences. They commented that people in the other countries wanted to engage in endless small talk about extraneous matters like families and hobbies. People were wonderful hosts and took the three Americans to some excellent restaurants, but conversations continued to focus on nonbusiness issues. All three managers had to renegotiate with travel agents since they were forced to extend their visits beyond their originally scheduled time frames.

Susan, Mike, and Judy are trying to do business in collectivist cultures. In these cultures, people view themselves as long-term members of a group. Given strong group affiliations, people benefit from group memberships but they also have extensive obligations to fellow members. With this combination of benefits and obligations, people in collectivist cultures do not offer group membership quickly. People want to feel that they can trust others within their groups and they are often suspicious of outsiders.

Potential collaborators and clients in the three countries want to learn a great deal about the three Americans. What sorts of people are they? Will they be good business partners? Can we trust them to follow through on commitments? Will they follow through on unwritten agreements that were sealed with a handshake? Answers to these questions come during the many conversations and evening dinners desired by members of collectivist cultures. If they agree to do business with the Americans, the people in the three countries would be offering collective memberships. This is a major step in business negotiations that collectivists take very seriously.

Americans certainly join many groups, but the time frame for membership is often shorter and the obligations are fewer. The three Americans who want to do business overseas have undoubtedly learned a set of social skills that allows them to meet people quickly and to get down to business. There is a different set of social skills in collectivist cultures that contribute to the message, "We value long-term commitments and realize that mutual trust is central to our relationships."

COMPLEXITY IN RELATIONSHIPS

Once the basics of individualism and collectivism are understood, people can analyze more complex intercultural encounters. One of the misunderstood aspects of collectivism is that groups are viewed as permanent. People do not bounce in and out of groups based on whims and personal changes. Given that the groups are permanent, members can set goals that are taken very seriously. If the goals demand that people speak up and disagree with each other, the image of the "harmonious collective" may seem to disappear.

Established Groups Can Set Norms for Various Work Behaviors

"I thought I was prepared for working in Japanese groups, but I was surprised by the level of vigorous discussion." Mike Cavanagh was sharing his observations in an e-mail message to hometown friends in Anacortes, Washington. Mike had been offered a six-month consultancy by Aoyama Music in Nagoya, Japan. Aoyama had a very good reputation for making harps and executives wanted to expand its product line with other acoustic instruments. Mike had a good reputation as a maker of various stringed instruments such as guitars, ukuleles, and mandolins.

Mike learned that he would be working with a group of managers who had been at Aoyama for over ten years and who knew each other well. Mike knew that Japan was a collectivist culture where people achieve much of their identity through group membership. He knew that in collectivist cultures people value politeness, cooperation, and a harmonious interaction style (Haugh, 2007). At meetings of the Aoyama workgroup, however, Mike found that team members argued vigorously, disagreed with each other, and were very forceful in putting their ideas forward.

Mike is correct about some basic aspects of collectivism and is now ready for more advanced material. In collective cultures, any one individual can have interactions with three categories of people. If the individual does not know other people, relations can be quite formal and "standoffish." People may have little to do with each other and can be rather abrupt and pushy if they come into contact in public places such as subway trains during rush hour. If the individual knows others but does not yet have collective ties with them, interactions can be very polite and guided by a complex system of etiquette. These people might be part of a collective in later years, and politeness is expected.

For long-term members of a collective, as in this example with Aoyama, people set norms to achieve various goals. If they have known each other for many years, collective membership has been established, and they don't need to always show carefully planned politeness. Instead, members may have set the norm that they need to argue vigorously about new products that will meet the demands of a fast-moving marketplace. They may not be a collective tomorrow if they don't formulate new ideas today!

In addition to understanding types of relations among people, individual differences must be taken into account. Culture provides general guidelines for behavior in a wide variety of social situations, but there will always be differences among people who find themselves in the same situations. For example, some Japanese individuals are more assertive and outspoken than others, and they may be among the first to voice public disagreements.

Understanding the distinction between individualism and collectivism assists in the analysis of problems in international business. For example, copyright law is much more developed, and copyrights much more respected, in some countries compared to others. One reason is that copyrights protect an individual's intellectual property, but as has been seen in previous incidents, some cultures place more emphasis on the individual than do other cultures.

Intellectual Property Rights Less Protected in Some Countries

As the author of well-received books on topics such as leadership and Asian economies, Michael LaPointe was a popular lecturer and business consultant. He was invited to give workshops in Shanghai at different companies contemplating expansion into international markets. His host was Wang Jun who had studied at UCLA and who heard Michael speak there six years ago. During a break from his hectic schedule, Michael suggested that they go to a department store so that he could buy gifts for friends and family members. In a section of one store that sold books, Michael found a Chinese version of his recently published *International Business and Your Future*. "I didn't know this version existed," Michael said. "Maybe protection of intellectual property will be better in future years," Wang Jun replied.

One reason for Michael's discovery of a pirated version of his book is based on a cultural difference. In China, historically, knowledge was considered open and that once a person made an intellectual contribution, others could use it. People using knowledge found in books and other publications did not have to constantly cite the sources of their ideas, as they must in individualistic countries such as the United States. In addition, the people who published would receive a great deal of status as "the author of a book." These select people did not feel the need for additional attention stemming from citations by others. As a colleague once told me, "The author has already achieved great prominence. It would be considered petty to insist on citations when others use published information. Further, the author should start a new book rather than waste time monitoring different versions of an earlier work."

There may be changes in the future. As part of entry into the World Trade Organization, the Chinese government has agreed to abide by the Trade-Related Aspects of Intellectual Property Rights agreement (TRIPs). This agreement provides a minimum level of protection for the owners of intellectual property. However, there are few judges and attorneys in

China familiar with intellectual property rights, and so there are now training programs being administered to develop the necessary expertise.

Another push for change is coming from individual Chinese authors, musicians, and fashion designers. These Chinese artists feel that they could do much better financially if there was protection against plagiarism, piracy, and knockoffs. Given that many have international followings, they have been successfully calling attention to the protection of their intellectual contributions.

As people become wealthier, their individualistic tendencies increase. One reason is that they want to protect their wealth, and another is that they have the resources to pursue their individual interests. As the economies of various countries, such as China, improve over the next twenty years, my prediction is that individualistic behavior will increase and old collective ties will weaken.

4

Communication: Interpreting Silence, Quiet, and Indirectness

When people live in other cultures, they will have countless opportunities to communicate with others. Some of these communications will be successful, some will be puzzling, and some will lead to misunderstandings. People's success during their sojourns will be largely dependent upon effective communication and the development of positive interpersonal relationships (Cushner & Brislin, 1996; Hall, 1959; Jandt, 1998).

Communication is the process where people exchange information, their emotions, and their behavioral intentions. The basic elements of communication can be pictured as follows.

Sender → noise → formation of message → noise

→ interpretation of message by receiver

For example, a sender telephones a friend to tell her about an ongoing party. There may literally be noise since other people at the party may be speaking loudly, making it hard for the sender to be heard. Other forms of noise may include the effort the sender is calling upon to formulate his message. He might be thinking, "I really don't know this woman all that well. I wonder what she will think when I call her about this party." The need to work through the additional noise brought on by these additional thoughts may have an impact on the informational aspect of the message. The sender may eventually say, "I was so concerned that I do not know her very well that I forgot to give the address of the party." There can also be noise during the interpretation of the message. The receiver may be holding down a conversation with someone in her apartment when she receives the call. There may be noise brought on by her thought processes. She might be thinking, "I wonder what he will think of me if I drop everything and come to this party." As a result of this effort, she may forget to write down the address of the party if the sender gives it to her.

This communication episode could take place when people are from the same cultural background, are the same age, have had similar life experiences, have similar amounts of formal education, and so forth. Still, the possibility exists that there will be communication errors. The potential number of errors is greater when people are participating in intercultural communications (Gibson & Zhong, 2005). During such interactions, people do not share the same cultural background. Some of the parties involved in the interaction may be using a second or third language. The people do not share the same communication norms that people learn as part of their socialization in a culture.

COMMUNICATION STYLES: SOFTNESS AND SUBTLETY

In this chapter, I will discuss what might be called the soft side of intercultural communication. Some communication difficulties are based on misinterpretations of soft interpersonal styles such as quiet, long periods of silence (Ikuko, 2006; Nakano, 2006), apologies rather than confrontations, lack of obvious emotional expressiveness, and subtle nonverbal signals (Molinsky, Krabbenhoft, Ambady, & Choi, 2005; Van de Vliert, 2007). "Style" refers to the manner in which people regularly communicate. Some people are regularly quiet and thoughtful. Others are loud, strident, and always can be depended upon for oral contributions during company meetings. Some people use very controlled, small body movements during their communications. Others are very demonstrative, using broad hand gestures and intense facial expressions. I have found it helpful to think about style by referring to different singers. Frank Sinatra and Elvis Presley make it on many lists of "my ten favorite singers," but they had very different styles when performing before live audiences.

There are different reasons people develop a communication style that they find useful. The contrast between a soft style (this chapter) and a more forceful and direct style (Chapter 5) is a good example. With a soft style, a boss can ask a subordinate, "I know your schedule is busy, but might you have the report done by Friday?" Or, the boss can say, "I want the report on my desk by Friday!"

There are at least four reasons for the difference. The first is that the choice of style is an aid in organizing knowledge. There are many ways people can behave, and the two communication styles help organize information on what good bosses do and how people in a culture should treat each other. A second reason is that the styles assist people in making decisions that others will accept. Many Americans living in Asia learn that they are much more productive if they adopt an indirect style. Asian businesspeople who spend time on the mainland United States learn that they must speak up in a direct manner or others will ignore them.

A third reason is that the styles can help people hide their shortcomings, which they do not want other people to recognize. If bosses have little to say about an issue, they can hide this fact with well-practiced soft and indirect comments. People with a direct style can sometimes hide their ignorance behind a speech filled with loudness and bluster. Finally, the styles can communicate people's values. With indirect comments, people are saying, "We respect others and know that they can make decisions on how to spend their workdays." With direct comments, people are saying, "It is important to let people know what bosses expect so that workers don't have to waste their valuable time with guessing games."

Difficulties are compounded when there are multiple cultural differences and when there are "moving targets." I have discussed just one difference here, but there can be a dozen aspects of culture encountered during the typical workweek. The concept of moving targets means that people may communicate softly or forcefully for one reason on Monday but for quite a different reason on Friday. Despite the admitted difficulties, the fact that we are in a fast-moving and multicultural world means that we must continually accept the challenges of understanding communications during intercultural interactions.

Let's examine a number of critical incidents that deal with soft aspects of intercultural communication. One of the most striking cultural differences is that people in some cultures are very comfortable with silence, while people in other cultures are very uncomfortable with silence and feel that it is a sign that communication is not proceeding well.

Silence Carries Culturally Influenced Meanings

"I hope people have more to say during the meeting to be held later today," Mark Tilden said to himself as he thought about ideas for improvements in the company where he worked. Mark had lived in Osaka, Japan, for one year. He worked as an editor and proofreader for a company that made parts for Japan's bullet trains. Some of the company's products were marketed in the United States and Australia, and

Mark reviewed English language materials prepared for use in those countries.

At the meeting, most people contributed little. Most of the meeting consisted of short reports from various division managers and others remained silent, even when questions were invited. Toward the end of the meeting's scheduled time, Mark made a suggestion that the company analyze recent developments in Amtrak scheduling in the Western United States. The company vice president, who was running the meeting, then told Mark to prepare a report on Amtrak within two weeks. Mark felt unprepared to take on this task.

There are cultural differences concerning reactions to silence. In the United States, people become uncomfortable with too much silence and speak up to fill empty space. I remember guides for proper teenager behavior that I read as an adolescent. One of the lessons was that, prior to a social engagement, people should find out what others are interested in talking about so that there is no uncomfortable silence. In Japan, people are much more comfortable with silence and there is no pressure to speak up to fill a void. Japanese children learn the adage, "Chinnmoku wa kin, yuuben wa gin." This translates as "Speech is silver, silence is golden." Given that silence is acceptable, people are likely to speak only when they have something to say. In this example, the company vice president may have felt that Mark knew a great deal about Amtrak and had been thinking about his potential contribution for months. Consequently, the vice president may have felt that asking Mark for a report in two weeks was quite reasonable.

Children in the United States often hear the adage, "Silence is golden." But the adage does not carry a strong lesson for everyday behavior as it does in Japan. In the United States, parents occasionally remind children of the adage when they are making too much noise. Or, adults sometimes use the adage in a sarcastic manner when someone is dominating a meeting in the workplace. When working in the United States, Japanese nationals often must adjust to expectations of greater participation in meetings. Human Resource Specialists sometimes offer training sessions during which Japanese nationals can practice speaking up and making contributions. If they don't speak up, American executives may feel that the Japanese have not "done their homework" prior to workplace meetings.

Beyond the Choice of Vocabulary. Nonverbal behaviors play a major role in intercultural communications. Nonverbal behaviors include all aspects of the communication beyond the choice of vocabulary. Nonverbal behaviors include facial expressions, body movements, choice of clothing, tone of voice, eye movements, and any other signals that people send and that might be interpreted correctly or incorrectly.

Albert Mehrabian (1968) made the case that total meaning conveyed and interpreted during face-to-face communication is 93 percent nonverbal. We don't have to accept Mehrabian's exact figure to work with the general idea that people's body movements, facial expressions, and voice tones are central in the communication process. This point is made in the following critical incident.

Nonverbal Behaviors Can Be Especially Difficult to Understand

In Japan, an American businessperson presents a proposal to a Japanese national concerning a potential joint venture. The American points to a paragraph that presents his thinking about marketing. The Japanese counterpart draws in his breath with a noise that sounds like "tssst," presents a serious expression on his face, and says that this aspect of the proposal needs special attention. The American concludes that his ideas about marketing are being looked upon favorably.

The misunderstanding here is that the American businessperson feels that the meeting has been successful but the Japanese counterpart feels that he has communicated that there are major difficulties. One reason is that the American is more likely to expect directness in communication. If the Japanese counterpart thought there was a problem, the American's expectation is that he would communicate this directly and in a forthright manner. In contrast, Japanese businesspeople often communicate in a more indirect style. The style is gentler, less confrontational, and less assertive. Phrases like "needs special attention" are meant to convey, in a gentle manner that there are difficulties. In addition, the nonverbal message that sounds like "tssst" is also a sign that the Japanese businessperson has identified difficulties. An equivalent nonverbal behavior among Americans would be raised eyebrows combined with a frown.

An indirect communication style is common throughout Asia and is looked upon favorably if sojourners are able to use it. I often advise American businesspeople who work in Asia to "tone down" their assertive and direct style in favor of a softer and harmony-seeking approach. I suggest that they think of a direct style as similar to two boxers trading punches and jabs. For an indirect style, a good image is two practitioners of Tai Chi facing each other and demonstrating slow and delicate arm movements.

Familiarity with an indirect style is not a guarantee of communication. Colleagues in Japan tell me, "We don't interpret indirectness correctly 100% of the time, even with people we have known for many years." Third parties are often called upon to clear up miscommunications. The third party knows and is trusted by the people involved and can have meetings with them to make sure that the original message has been communicated as clearly as possible.

Apologies and Silence. Another type of soft communication is the use of apologies. In some cultures, people are much more likely to apologize if they are part of accidents or misunderstandings than are people in cultures where communication is more forceful and direct.

Apologies: Different Meanings across Cultures

Harumi Tanaka, from Osaka, Japan, had accepted an assignment in Boston. His task was to explore the possibility of developing joint ventures with American firms. He had been invited by one company to spend a month and had been assigned an office and a research assistant. He agreed on a Monday to present a business plan the following Friday. On Tuesday, the computers in the company crashed and the research assistant called in sick with a severe case of flu. Still, Harumi pushed forward and presented his plan on Friday. He began his presentation, "I'm sorry that I am not well prepared. This meeting may not be a good use of your time." He then went into a clear, interesting presentation. After the meeting, one of the American executives said, "I don't know why you had to apologize. Everyone knows about the computer crash and your assistant's illness." Harumi responded that he thought that the apology would be a good introduction to his presentation.

The misunderstanding in this incident occurred because apologies are interpreted differently in the United States compared to Japan. In the United States, apologies are associated with weakness and with the admission of guilt. In this case, people at the meeting might interpret Harumi's apology as an admission of responsibility for a poor presentation. In Japan, apologies are less associated with weakness or with the admission of guilt. Apologies show concern for the difficulties and emotional distress people are experiencing. However, Japanese people making apologies are not necessarily claiming that they are responsible for the difficulties or distress.

Japanese like hearing apologetic language. It shows modesty and demonstrates that people are not putting themselves above others. A Japanese colleague told me, "We enjoy hearing the language of apologies, much like we enjoy hearing the breeze as it moves through palm trees." Before my first lecture tour in Japan, a wise colleague advised me to use phrases such as "I hope there is something in this lecture that is worthwhile. Many of you in the audience could make a better presentation." A comparable type of language Americans like to hear deals with compliments. Examples are, 'That suggestion you made in the meeting was excellent," or "I appreciate your hard work on the recently completed project."

Differing views about apologies is one reason for bitterness among the families of sailors who died in the collision between the Ehime Maru and the USS Greeneville. The two ships were from Japan and the United States, respectively, and they collided near Hawaii in February 2001. The Ehime Maru was a Japanese training ship, and nine young sailors lost their lives. The Japanese family members wanted to hear timely apologies that would have indicated the deep regret, concern, and empathy of Americans involved in the collision. American Naval officials delayed their apologies because (before examination of the cultural differences) they felt they would be admitting their guilt and would be exposing themselves to career-ending judicial proceedings and to lawsuits.

The Japanese families, then, expected apologies but instead received silence. Differing expectations about what verbal expressions should occur, and the substitution of silence, is central to understanding this incident.

More Than One Interaction during the Day

Mary Collins had impressed her superiors during her five years at the Pittsburgh office of a manufacturing firm specializing in farm equipment. Her superiors asked her to accept an assignment in Russia to determine the possibility of joint ventures. A firm in Moscow was identified whose executives agreed to have a series of meetings with Mary. On her first day at the firm, she met Yuri Sakharov, who showed her around, introduced her to secretaries, and offered to answer questions as they came up during the next few weeks.

The next morning, Mary saw Yuri in the hall and they greeted each other and had a short conversation. Later in the afternoon, Mary saw Yuri again but he walked by her and did not acknowledge her presence. Mary wondered if she had done or said something offensive earlier in the day.

The cultural issue here involves a difference in workplace norms regarding how people are expected to respond to each other over the course of the day. In the United States, there is often the informal norm that people acknowledge each other every time they come into contact. In Russia, the norm is that "once is enough." People greet each other and exchange pleasantries the first time they see each other, but they are not expected to do this upon a second or third meeting during the same day. Mary should not take the lack of a second greeting personally. Yuri is behaving quite appropriately according to Russian workplace norms.

My colleague Julia Nikulina Compton is originally from Siberia and has also worked in Moscow. She points to another implication of the American desire to chat at every interaction compared to the "once is enough" norm.

Julia has had the opportunity to learn a number of languages other than her native Russian. She found English the easiest of these additional languages to learn. She points out that "English speakers, especially Americans, are willing to talk with you and so you have the opportunity to get a lot of practice."

If speakers of other languages don't feel the need to have conversations with people more than once a day, there is far less opportunity for everyday use of language. Teachers of second languages always give students the advice to move beyond their textbooks and to engage native speakers in as many conversations as possible.

Differing expectations about "speaking up" contrasted with being silent is a problem at workplace meetings attended by people from different cultural backgrounds.

Speaking Up in Public: What Purposes Are Served?

"Why didn't you speak up at the luncheon meeting?" Anne Jackson asked Seiko Tanaka. "The people were discussing savings rates among Japanese wage earners and I've heard you talk about this before. You are better informed than the others, but you said very little."

Anne and Seiko had just returned to their offices after a luncheon meeting in Honolulu. Anne, originally from Nashville, Tennessee, had lived in Hawaii for five years. Seiko was from Osaka, Japan, and had accepted a job in Hawaii with a Japanese-owned chain of department stores. Anne and Seiko shared an interest in American country music and had lunch together every two or three weeks. Anne was impressed with Seiko's knowledge of Japanese consumer behavior, family savings plans, and the roles of husbands and wives in raising children.

At the luncheon with coworkers from company headquarters, one of the executives offered conclusions about Japanese family savings that Anne recognized as quite different from ideas held by Seiko. Anne expected Seiko to speak up, but Seiko quietly said, "You have an interesting perspective." Even when Anne encouraged her to share her ideas, Seiko added only that "different people have diverse opinions about complex issues such as Japanese consumer behavior."

The cultural difference in this incident centers on the distinction between privately held positions and publicly expressed opinions. Anne comes from a culture where the distinction is less pronounced than in Seiko's culture. To Anne, if people have a private opinion in the workplace, and if sharing that opinion could enrich a discussion, then the person should speak up and share the opinion with others. To Seiko, there can be a sharp distinction between privately held opinions (in Japanese, "honne") and public presentations of the self ("tatemae"). Seiko can be quite comfortable holding a strong opinion but not telling others about it.

Reasons are often based on interpersonal concerns and sensitivities. Seiko may feel that she will interfere with the pleasant interactions among people at the lunch if she offers her disagreements. Her concerns about maintaining positive interpersonal relationships may take precedence over her need to express her well-thought-out opinions.

Dating couples sometimes encounter this difference. A Japanese woman asked for my advice on a problem she was having with her American boyfriend. The boyfriend complained, "You are always so nice and never disagree or complain when we are with others!" My advice was to suggest that the boyfriend be thankful for the good fortune of knowing a woman who is polite (Haugh, 2007) and sensitive to the needs of others.

Preparing for the Possibility of a Frustrating Silence. People in some cultures are so uncomfortable with silence that they say something just to fill a void. People in cultures where silence is common know this cultural difference and sometimes remain silent, hoping that their business partners seeking joint ventures will say something that takes the form of a concession during the bargaining process. Since silence can be interpreted as disinterest, people are uncomfortable with silence and may keep saying things until they think they recognize a flicker of interest coming from their conversational partners. If they continue to receive silence, they may mistakenly conclude they have not found interested partners and may take their business elsewhere.

If people know that silence may frustrate some potential business partners, they sometimes can take steps to deal with this possibility, as in this incident.

Listening to the Thundering Thud of Silence

"Hong Kong beckons," Jed Poole said to himself as he made final arrangements for his first trip to Asia. Jed was a very successful telecommunications executive in Miami and had been invited to Hong Kong to examine possible joint ventures. Chiu Xing, president of a small company whose board of directors wanted to expand into other Asian markets, initiated the visit. Jed told Chiu Xing that he would like to give a talk to company employees and to make suggestions for future collaborative activities. He shared a few preliminary ideas on specific projects during e-mail exchanges with Chiu Xing, who then asked various managers to do research on these ideas.

After arriving in Hong Kong and meeting with company executives, Jed was led to a room where he would give his presentation. Approximately fifty employees attended, including recently hired managers from Thailand, Japan, and Vietnam. Jed thought that he did a good job, but when he asked for questions or comments he was met with a deafening silence.

This contrasted greatly with the feistiness and intellectual give-and take-he was accustomed to at meetings in Miami.

Jed has encountered a cultural guidance for behavior that is common in Asia. People don't often ask questions or share reactions after a formal presentation. One explanation is that, from the Asian perspective, the disadvantages of questions and comments outweigh the advantages. Company employees may feel that they will look foolish if their question or comments are too elementary. They may be especially sensitive about this given that people from different countries are present and so national pride may be a factor. They may fear that they will be indirectly criticizing Chiu Xing for not preparing them well enough for Jed's visit. They may even feel that Jed will be insulted if there is the indirect suggestion that he should have covered other material in his formal presentation.

If Chiu Xing wants questions and answers, he must give people preparation time for this task. He may know that Americans often end their talks with the inquiry, "Any questions?" With this knowledge, he can ask employees to prepare questions and comments as part of their research prior to Jed's visits. He can let five or six employees know that he will be calling on them after Jed's presentation. As long as people are prepared and have been encouraged to ask questions and to make suggestions, they are willing to go beyond the stony silence that often marks the end of formal presentations.

Interpreting Subtle Signals. People from cultures where silence is common learn to interpret subtle signals that coworkers give. People learn that others do not always express their feelings about company issues by verbalizing them. Rather, they communicate their feelings through body language and facial expressions, or through the choice of the few words that they choose to use.

Getting the Message: Who Is Responsible?

"If the vice president set a new policy, I do not understand what it is," Susan Tyler told Kanya Chaisee as they left a staff meeting. Susan and Kanya worked for American Express in Bangkok, Thailand, and they had just attended a meeting where the vice president was to announce changes in policies concerning personal credit cards. Susan was originally from Austin, Texas, and Kanya had spent her entire life in Thailand. Kanya told Susan, "I thought Mr. Ittiporn, the vice president, was very clear. Customers now have various choices concerning how they will pay their credit card balance."

The different reactions expressed by Susan and Kanya reflect a cultural difference in the relationship between the sender and the recipient of communications. In the United States, the person who wants to communicate a message has the responsibility for seeing that this goal is accomplished. The person is expected to be clear, well-organized, and should deliver the message in an interesting and enthusiastic manner. Institutions in the United States offer ways of developing these communication skills. Public speaking is a required course in many high schools and in most colleges. People learn to stand on their feet, to be the focus of an audience's attention, and to deliver their messages clearly.

In Thailand, the responsibility for successful communication is shared among senders and recipients. Even if the speaker is dull, unclear, and unorganized, the recipients are expected to invest energy into understanding the message. This means that they must listen carefully, consider other presentations speakers have made for hints on how they indicate important points, and be sensitive to cues from nonverbal sources such as facial expressions and body language. Given that she has learned to listen carefully and to interpret subtle cues, Kanya is quite confident that she was able to interpret Mr. Ittiporn's decisions about credit card policies.

There are parallel sets of advice for people who will be living and working in another culture. If they plan to work in the United States, Thais should consider taking a course in public speaking. Before accepting a job assignment in Thailand and many other Asian countries, Americans should practice skills such as paying attention to speakers and considering their nonverbal cues. Adult education programs in community colleges sometimes offer courses called "listening skills" which can be very useful.

Showing Appreciation. Some soft conversational conventions serve important aspects of a culture. The distinction between individualism and collectivism was discussed in Chapter 3. In collectivist cultures, group membership is highly valued and is considered permanent. In individualistic cultures, people move from group to group as their goals and interests change. This leads to different communication norms. People in individualistic cultures want their contributions to others recognized with words of appreciation. People in collectivist cultures do not feel the need to verbalize their appreciation to members of their groups, since everyone already knows that they are grateful to each other.

When Is a "Thank You" in the Workplace Expected?

"One little word is 'thank you' and another little word is 'please'!" This song that used to be played on a children's television show kept going through Sharon Colson's mind. Sharon worked in Los Angeles for an accounting firm. She was a good public speaker and was often invited by colleges to give presentations on the day-to-day work of accountants.

Since she liked working with business students, her boss asked her to look after the college interns her company sponsored.

One of the interns was Dong Soo Park from Pusan, South Korea. He felt comfortable talking with Sharon and they would have lunch together at Korean restaurants. One day, he confided in Sharon that he had fallen in love with an American woman and that they hoped to settle in California or Arizona. He asked Sharon to write some letters of recommendation for him as part of his job search. These requests came at the rate of three or four a month, and Sharon was conscientious about meeting the deadlines indicated in the various job announcements. What Sharon missed was any acknowledgement of the hours she spent on these letters and any words such as "thank you" from Dong Soo.

Sharon has encountered a cultural difference concerning the use of phrases like "thank you." In Korea, these phrases are used more often with people who do not know each other well. Once people spend time together and become close, they assume that favors and positive behaviors are appreciated. If they had to say "thank you" frequently, this would be a sign that the relationship is not particularly close. Dong Soo thinks of Sharon as someone close, as indicated by their shared lunch hours and by the fact that he confided to her about his girlfriend.

In the United States, people expect to be thanked and appreciated each time they help someone else. The social necessity of showing appreciation is part of childhood socialization, as indicated by the television theme song that Sharon remembered. There are individual Koreans who will be attentive to American expectations concerning appreciation. They may have seen enough American movies and television shows to learn this cultural difference. Or, they may have read an American etiquette book or a magazine article with a title like, "Showing Appreciation for Workplace Favors." This is a cultural difference where my advice is, "Americans should expect less verbal appreciation, Koreans should try to offer more, and hopefully they will meet in the middle."

5

Communication: Interpreting Directness and Potentially Negative Exchanges

In this chapter, the central role that communication plays in the success, or lack thereof, of sojourns will continue. In contrast to the soft, quiet, and indirect (Schouten, 2007) communication styles reviewed in Chapter 4, this chapter deals with direct styles that are sometimes interpreted as insensitive and harsh. Special problems occur when communicators do not mean to be negative, but receivers interpret their verbal and nonverbal behavior as personally directed and motivated by anger or disappointment.

Most people go through their work days expecting positive things to happen to them. In addition, they know what happiness is and they seek it during their everyday experiences (Diener 2000, Fredrickson & Losada, 2005). If they don't seek such positive behaviors and happiness, this can be a symptom of depression and the need to seek professional help from mental health counselors.

A DIRECT COMMUNICATION STYLE

Part of people's socialization in a culture is learning how to communicate effectively with others. Communication serves people's goals. People want social interactions, good jobs, formal education that serves their interests, opportunities to pursue hobbies, and so forth. All of these involve the presence of others in their lives with whom they need to communicate so as to form positive interpersonal relations. Part of the communication process is people's style, or the manner in which they communicate. People in some cultures learn to be very direct and to speak their minds openly. These people choose a very colorful and clear vocabulary when they speak, and they use forceful body movements and a firm tone of voice. When they communicate using this style, they are prepared to have receivers respond in a similar manner. People familiar with and comfortable with the style feel that communication efficiency is enhanced. They say, "Let's not beat around the bush trying to be lighthearted with each other. We don't have all day—let's cut the small talk and get down to business! Respect my ability to deal with a direct communication style, and I'll show respect for you by behaving in the same way."

But not all cultures socialize people to deal with this direct and straightforward style. In many parts of Asia, for example, a softer style marks a polite and well-mannered individual who knows how to maintain harmony in groups (Haugh, 2007; Ting-Toomey, 1985). Outsiders, such as sojourners, who enter a social situation with their firm opinions and willingness to disagree are seen as barbaric. In addition to maintaining harmony, another reason for an indirect style should be mentioned. In cultures where hierarchy and respect for powerful people are prominent, an indirect style serves the goals of bosses and executives. If subordinates do not use a direct and forceful style while interacting with them, bosses feel that they are receiving deference. If outsiders use a straightforward style, executives may feel that their status is being challenged.

Many of the critical incidents to be discussed in this chapter deal with differing expectations. One person in the communication process expected positive encounters but interpreted interactions with others as problematic and negative. As previously mentioned, people expect that positive things will happen to them. Given this expectation, negative encounters have more impact than positive encounters. Imagine a company where a worker interacts frequently with her boss. The boss has almost always been positive and there have been 100 interactions where the boss gave positive feedback. But one day, the boss tells his subordinate that he is disappointed with a recent project report. Does the worker combine the encounter involving one piece of negative feedback with the 100 previous positive interactions and walk away with positive feelings? Or does the negative impact have a special impact, leading to negative feelings? The second response is more probable: a few negative interactions can overwhelm the positive feelings generated by a much larger number of positive interactions. This is a special problem in intercultural encounters where people do not mean to be negative, but others interpret their behavior as rude and uncaring. This can be seen in this incident, where a Russian visitor to the United States thought he was being helpful, but his American hosts considered his behavior as insensitive and unthinking.

Direct Questions Sometimes Yield Direct Answers

"Almost the entire business community became involved in fundraising efforts to purchase our concert grand piano," Deborah Madden told Vladimir Petrov as they entered the auditorium in Pennebrook, Washington. Vladimir was an internationally renowned pianist from St. Petersburg, Russia, who had agreed to present a concert in the community's music series. Deborah was the owner of a department store, had studied Russian for four years in college, and thought she could help with Vladimir's visit. Residents of Pennebrook were proud of their reputation as a small community with a big city's offerings in art, music, dance, and theater.

After the well-received concert, Vladimir attended a reception organized by the directors of the music series. He was asked, "What do you think of our grand piano?" Vladimir responded that while the piano manufacturer had a prestigious name, he found the workmanship on this specific piano to be substandard. "Also, the tone is imprecise and the fingering makes difficult passages almost impossible to play well." Deborah's jaw dropped as she heard this, but she felt that she had to translate Vladimir's comments as accurately as she could. After hearing the comments, attendees at the reception found it difficult to engage Vladimir in further conversations.

The cultural difference is that in some cultures, people give direct responses to direct questions. This is especially true when people are asked about areas of expertise, as in this example with Vladimir and the quality of concert pianos. People share the advice, "If you don't want a straightforward answer, don't ask a question." This incident and analysis developed from conversations with Julia Nikulina Compton, University of Hawaii, Kapiolani. She is from Novosibirsk, Siberia, and has also worked in Moscow. Most of the books that describe cultural differences say that Americans are very direct in their communications (Hall, 1959, 1966). But there are many exceptions. When people's feelings might be hurt, Americans who place a premium on smooth social skills frequently tone down their answers to questions. A socially skilled American pianist might say, "The manufacturer chose an excellent type of wood for the piano." The American is saying something positive without giving a complete analysis of the piano.

I once asked Julia, "You know Russian culture extremely well. Have you changed your behavior now that you are in the United States?" She replied, "I smile a lot more. I can often communicate the same message as I would in Moscow, such as 'No, you can't turn in your report late!' But I do this with a smile and pleasant voice tone. I have few problems when I communicate this way."

Mixing Direct and Indirect Styles. Another cultural difference is that people in some cultures know how to be direct, but they limit this behavior to the workday. During evening social encounters and during weekend interactions in their communities, they are much softer and indirect in their communications. The question, "When are we direct and when are we softer" is central to analyzing this incident.

Communication during Work and Leisure Time

Bob Fletcher, originally from Chicago, was working in Frankfurt, Germany, for an international pharmaceutical company. One of his colleagues was Dieter Kornadt, who had recently joined the company after receiving an advanced degree in psychology from a German university. Bob and Dieter had been assigned the task of developing a creative marketing plan for the sale of over-the-counter pain relievers. Bob's college degree was in art history and he had taken courses where professors applied research on the creative process to specific works of art.

Bob and Dieter worked well together and one evening agreed to have a few pints at a nearby beer garden. Knowing about Dieter's recent advanced degree, Bob tried to introduce some light conversation about major European composers and various aspects of their personal lives. Dieter contributed to the discussion with detailed analyses of Beethoven and his personality, deafness, home life, and disappointments in his romantic relationships. Bob thought to himself, "I wish this guy would lighten up!"

Bob is experiencing cultural differences in the relationship between work and leisure time spent with the same person. In the United States, many people make a sharp distinction and friends and family members will criticize them if they "talk shop" too much at nonwork gatherings. In Germany, the boundary between work and leisure time is fuzzier. Many Germans engage in intense and analytical discussions after work. In Dieter's mind, the beer hall discussion was work related. He and Bob were working on a creative marketing plan, creativity was a part of the evening discussion, and so his serious approach to work could continue.

Dieter's intense approach to work also includes judging the capabilities of his colleague and deciding whether to request other joint job assignments. If Bob fails to converse in a detailed and analytical manner during after-hours gatherings, Dieter may conclude that Bob is an intellectual lightweight who is unworthy of serious attention.

A related issue is that Germans often continue their professional identities into their weekend activities. For example, if they are hiking in the forest or visiting the zoo with friends, they continue to make conversation based on their identities as engineers, psychologists, physicians, or economists. In preparing for an assignment in Germany, Americans should prepare for serious discussions in topic areas such as arts and culture, politics, and important historical events.

Insights into One's Own Culture. We must constantly keep in mind that everyone is influenced by the culture in which they are socialized. It is relatively easy to observe the dress styles, eating habits, and music of people from other cultures and have something to say when asked about cultural differences. It is harder to examine oneself and to answer the question, "What is there about my own culture that affects my behavior?" In this incident, a businessperson from Hong Kong must adjust to a collection of communication norms that has developed in big cities within the United States. I hope that Americans who read this incident will remember encounters in their own lives that are similar to the one depicted here and in so doing will obtain some insights into their own culture.

Efficient Social Interactions Can Seem Rude

Peter Chiu, from Hong Kong, was a wholesaler in precious gems. He traveled to Washington, DC, to make inquiries about pending legislation concerning import quotas. He had attended college with Beth Reardon, who was now a congressional aide on Capitol Hill. Beth invited Peter to attend a fund-raiser for a prominent senator.

Upon arriving at the fund-raiser, Peter was given a nametag. He knew that he should try to circulate among the various attendees, and he began this task. Some people would walk up to him, look at his nametag, and then walk away. Others would begin talking with him but after about fifteen seconds would do an "about face" and leave to talk with someone else. People told him they had to leave shortly since they had four other social gatherings to attend that evening. Peter had never encountered behaviors like these and felt ignored and disrespected.

Beth seems unaware that there are communication norms in Washington, DC, about which Peter may not be knowledgeable. Culture provides guidance for shared behaviors among people seeking similar goals. The behaviors eventually become "proper and acceptable" if people who practice them increase their success rate in attaining their goals. For example, many people share the goal of honoring high school graduates. The shared behavior in Hawaii is that friends and relatives present graduates with flower leis at the reception following the graduation ceremony. This behavior is rare in other parts of the United States.

Peter's reactions might be less negative if he understands the goals that people have. Many attendees at the fundraiser want to pursue various lobbying efforts or want to improve the legislation on which they are working. In Washington, DC, people have agreed to share certain behaviors that are admittedly rude in most other parts of the United States. Attendees admit this and modify these behaviors when visiting other cities. People look at someone else's nametag. If that other person is not working for an organization related to current lobbying and legislative efforts, people move on to someone else. Chatting with people for fifteen seconds and leaving abruptly serves the same goal. In this short period of time, attendees can determine if someone else will be useful or not. If the shared behavior of "many social gatherings in the same evening" is considered acceptable, then people can go to different events in the hopes of finding someone who can contribute to their current work projects.

The Role of Enthusiasm. Other forms of a soft contrasted with intense communication style can occur when people meet each for the first time. People welcome each other in an enthusiastic manner. Does this have special meaning for the person being welcomed, or is it the way that people behave with everyone?

Enthusiastic Welcomes Can Have Complex Implications

Wang Ming, from Nanjing, worked for a Chinese-United States joint venture that manufactured cell phones. He accepted an assignment at company headquarters in Atlanta. Dave Jarrell had traveled extensively throughout China during the negotiation phase of the joint venture. The company president asked Dave to meet with Ming to welcome him to Atlanta and to his new assignment.

Dave met with Ming and greeted him in a pleasant, enthusiastic manner. He asked Ming about his trip and if he had settled into Atlanta yet. He offered to introduce Ming to a real estate agent for an apartment or house search. He also advised Ming to make sure that he had a new computer in his office. "We ordered some new ones and there are plenty to go around, so make sure you are not stuck with last generation's technology."

Ming clearly enjoyed the meeting and thanked Dave for his kind welcome. About two weeks later, Ming called Dave and asked for two favors. One was advice on renegotiating his salary, and the other was a request for his own personal secretary. Dave became mildly upset with these requests and wondered why Ming had chosen him to become involved in these negotiations.

The cultural difference here is whether or not an enthusiastic and charming interaction style is directed at many people, or whether these behaviors are limited to a select few people. In the United States, individuals use an enthusiastic style with many people. If they don't use such a style, they may be labeled "cold fish" who never learned their social skills. In China and other Asian countries, people can be charming and animated in their interpersonal interactions. However, they often limit these behaviors to a smaller number of people. When they behave in an enthusiastic manner, they are signaling a willingness to form a special relationship.

In this incident, Ming interpreted Dave's behavior as indicating special attention. Ming thought that Dave would be an important professional mentor and so felt comfortable discussing salary and secretarial support. Dave was behaving as he would with virtually all workplace interactions. "I'm using the social skills my mother taught me," he might say. Consequently, Dave is surprised when Ming makes his requests just two weeks after their first meeting. To prepare people for these very different interpretations, Human Resource Specialists at the company should offer cross-cultural training programs for all people who will be involved in intercultural interactions, not just the employees from overseas.

If people are accustomed to being greeted in an enthusiastic manner, they may interpret a staid style as a sign of rejection. This incident deals with a situation that contrasts with the previous incident. Here, an American who is familiar with showing enthusiasm does not find it during a trip to Asia.

Initial Reactions to Proposals during Business Trips

Traveling from her home near San Francisco, California, Karen Burke represented her computer manufacturing company on a sales trip to three Asian countries.

Karen traveled to Japan, Korea, and China, and made stops in several large cities within each country. Her goal was to introduce innovative technologies that had proven very popular in American and Canadian markets. Arriving back at company headquarters, she reported that she experienced limited success on this trip, her first to Asia. "People listened attentively, but I did not feel that they were anywhere near as enthusiastic as people were on my recent trip to the Eastern United States."

Karen has experienced cultural differences in the role that enthusiastic interactions play in the development of interpersonal and business relationships. In the United States, people learn to meet others in an enthusiastic manner as part of social skills development. While growing up, they are taught to meet people quickly and to put them at ease, to show interest in what they have to say, to keep up conversations on a variety of topics, and to tell them how much they enjoyed the interactions. I remember my mother shooing me out of the house to go to the birthday parties of junior high school classmates. "You have to learn to meet people and to make them feel comfortable interacting with you," she insisted, and she was correct.

In many other parts of the world, enthusiastic reactions when meeting others for the first time are not expected. Rather, people are more wary and careful and want to get to know others well before communicating special interest and a clear desire for future interactions. Karen needs to view her first trip to Asia as part of a long-term investment and should be happy that people were attentive when she talked about new technologies.

Later, if she feels that people are taking a special interest in her and her products, she can view this as a positive development in her business relationships in the three Asian countries.

The cultural difference leads to predictable reactions. To Americans, many Asians seem like "cold fish" and as rather dry and dull. To Asians, many Americans seem superficial given that they offer equal enthusiasm to everyone they meet. If Asians misinterpret American exuberance as indicating special attention, they may be disappointed if the Americans do not follow through with other offers of friendship or positive business relationships.

There will be individual differences among people, and these should always be kept in mind when cultural differences are discussed. There are individual Asians who meet people in a vivacious manner, and there are Americans who are dour and sour. Cultural differences exist, but people should always keep in mind that they will encounter exceptions when they travel extensively in other countries.

Self-Promotion. Enthusiasm rather than wariness becomes part of people's communication arsenal. People who have been successful with forthright practices such as showing enthusiasm quickly often make mistakes in other cultures where a softer style is preferred. This can be especially true of people comfortable with a direct style who are from individualistic cultures. People in individualistic cultures have to learn to engage in self-promotion since there is no automatic support group whose members take on this task. I remember my father telling me, "You've got to learn to blow your own horn, or there is the danger that no one else will do it." But blowing your own horn is considered distasteful in many cultures.

Discussing Strengths Left to Others in Some Cultures

Kevin Atkins had been invited to a Korean multinational organization in Kwanju to discuss the possibility of establishing a joint venture. Kevin, from Los Angeles, was a successful entrepreneur who had started several companies in the petrochemical industry. Upon arrival in Kwanju, he was met by the organization's vice president, Sun-Woo Park.

After becoming settled and meeting several other top executives at a dinner gathering, Kevin made his final modifications to the presentation he would make at the company.

After Sun-Woo Park's introduction that reviewed his impressive record, Kevin began his presentation by pointing out possibilities for the future that would build upon past successes. He said, "I think we can do business together. If you look at my business history, you will see a collection of successes and accomplishments. You will see evidence of my innovativeness, ability to spot opportunities, and the skills necessary to turn plans into reality." Kevin continued with these themes for about five more minutes. As he paused to look at his audience, however, he felt that people showed less enthusiasm at that moment compared to the beginning of his presentation.

Kevin has encountered a cultural difference concerning the description of one's personal abilities and accomplishments. In the United States, it is acceptable for people to describe themselves in a positive manner. Self-promotion can be overdone in any country, but in the United States there are ways of talking about oneself that stop short of bragging. There are fewer acceptable ways in Korea. Modesty, and not calling special attention to oneself, is looked upon far more favorably.

Koreans point to a proverb that they learn as children. "The mature rice plant bows down lower." This means that the more knowledge or wisdom people have, the more humble they should be. Koreans typically think of braggarts as immature and superficial. Compared to people who are humble, those who brag are also seen as less knowledgeable and intelligent.

How should Kevin communicate his accomplishments and abilities? He should leave this task to others. If the organization's vice president is hosting Kevin and introduces his presentation, then a "stamp of approval" has clearly been made. Sun-Woo Park made references to Kevin's past successes. Especially in a country like Korea where executives are expected to be especially attentive to a vice president's remarks, enough positive information on Kevin has been communicated. He can now emphasize the substantive aspects of his proposal for a joint venture.

Being Alert to Culture-Specific Styles. To be successful on sojourns, people clearly have to be sensitive to cultural norms regarding communication styles and practices. There are many cultural differences within any one country such as the United States. I have lived in Hawaii for over thirty years, and this incident captures the puzzlement of newcomers from mainland United States who encounter the communication practice known as "talk story." If people know and use this practice, it leads to collaboration rather than a direct communication of one's viewpoints.

"Let's Talk Story": An Invitation to Collaborate

Given his deep interest in public policy, Jim Rogers wanted to become involved in legislative issues after his move to Hawaii from Hartford, Connecticut. In college, he had majored in sociology and took as many courses in gerontology as he could. He visited the Hawaii state Capitol and spoke with various lobbyists. He was especially intrigued after discussions with Karen Nagato, who represented a group of people interested in insurance programs focusing on long-term care for the elderly. This group was giving special attention to programs for the frail elderly who needed round-the-clock nursing home care.

Jim had been an effective lobbyist back in Connecticut but he was not pleased with his ability to communicate with legislators in Hawaii. One day, he overheard Karen talking with a state senator in the hallway, and the senator ended the conversation with the suggestion, "Let's get together again and talk story!" Karen seemed very pleased with this invitation but Jim was clueless about what the senator meant.

"Talk story" is a style of communication in Hawaii that emphasizes shared meanings and experiences among people who have or want to develop a strong relationship. Conversations among people resemble a story, with characters, a plot line, details on what happened to people, and an ending. Participants in talk story focus on experiences that are familiar and that will elicit signs of recognition from people listening to the story. The goal is to develop or to reinforce a sense of "we" rather than "I" during conversations.

When talking story with a legislator, for example, Karen would try to find shared experiences and concerns. She might mention how her family had to dip into college savings accounts for her younger brothers so that they could pay the costs of nursing home care for her grandmother. The legislator might reply that her family was frustrated since insurance was so expensive to the point of unaffordable, even though her mother was currently a healthy sixty-year-old. The important point is that they are sharing stories about concerns and experiences, not on details such as "co-payments" and "time limits."

Efforts to address these necessary details will be made easier after talk story sessions that assist in relationship development.

Careful listening is an important part of talk story. Sometimes, stories are indirect and elliptical and so people have to listen carefully to discover the speaker's concerns and priorities. When people listen carefully, of course, they reap added benefits from showing respect to their communication partners.

CULTURAL SCRIPTS

Some mistakes during intercultural communications are hard to diagnose. Striking examples of such difficulties occur when people behave in a manner that they consider socially skilled and lighthearted, but that others interpret as much more forceful and full of meaning.

Violating Expectations during Business Meetings Can Affect Negotiations

Traveling to the United States to investigate investment possibilities, two Japanese investors contacted various state agencies that assisted small businesses. The investors asked people in the agencies about entrepreneurs who were willing to share their business plans. In one state, the agency official contacted several businesspeople and asked them if they would like to make a presentation to the Japanese visitors. Taking advantage of this opportunity, the official also asked other local investors if they wanted to attend. After introductions and a warm welcome by the agency's executive director, two of the American entrepreneurs began a joint presentation that described their plans for a software development organization.

Several of the people in the audience knew the speakers. These audience members asked lighthearted questions and kidded the speakers concerning their use of an old version of Power Point. "If you are proposing the latest in software, why are you using the technology of three years ago in your presentation?" one asked in a humorous effort to keep the meeting pleasant. During a break in the presentation, the people who knew each other discussed their golf scores and their favorite baseball teams. The two Japanese visitors were silent during the second half of the presentation. They left the meeting and the agency officials never heard from them again. The officials thought that the entrepreneurs made a good presentation and wondered why the Japanese did not respond in a more positive manner.

One reason for the poor reception is that the Americans violated a cultural script. Based on research by Yale University's Robert Abelson (1981), scripts refer to collections of behaviors that people use to accomplish their goals. Scripts have a beginning, a middle, and an end and involve sequences of behaviors that become familiar to members of a culture. In Hawaii, part of the script after arriving at someone's home is to take off one's shoes. At an organization's meeting of all employees, executives present guest speakers with leis. When a child is one-year-old, part of the celebration script is to hold a luau. These behaviors are not often part of home visits, wedding receptions, and one-year-old birthday parties in other states.

The Americans at the meeting were unaware of the Japanese visitors' expectations. In Japan, meetings where entrepreneurs present business plans are serious matters. People behave in very reserved ways and there is no place for humor or lighthearted remarks (Bell, 2007; Rogerson-Revell, 2007). In contrast, the Americans knew each other prior to the meeting and felt that a few jokes and kidding remarks would be appropriate. In disagreeing, the Japanese felt that the Americans were not serious about their business plans. They would argue, "If the businesspeople joke so much, will they be careful and diligent with investments that we might make?"

When dealing with people from other cultural backgrounds, it is often wise to ask, "What script am I in? Do people in other cultures expect a set of behaviors that might be different than those I intended to demonstrate?" People who have lived in another culture, such as Japanese nationals who have had overseas assignments, are often good informants when such questions are posed to them.

6

Dealing with Criticisms and Disagreements

INTRODUCTION: CHALLENGES TO PEOPLE'S ATTITUDES AND SELF IMAGES

People who are in a position to have extensive intercultural interactions often have had success in their own cultures. They have the education and professional experience to be chosen for positions such as overseas representative of a company, diplomat, or technical assistance adviser. If they enroll at an overseas university as part of their education, they usually have a good academic record and letters of recommendations from educators with whom they have worked. All these qualifications mean that people who engage in intercultural interactions have healthy self-images. They are confident that they can set goals and engage in the behaviors necessary to attain them.

During their intercultural interactions, however, they are likely to encounter challenges to their self-images. Sojourners cannot possibly be prepared to discuss all issues that host nationals consider important. Consequently, sojourners will feel frustrated if they cannot keep up conversations in the presence of hosts. They will find that hosts disagree with them on many issues since the hosts are likely to bring very different perspectives to discussions of important topics. Sojourners, even with the best of intentions, are also likely to engage in behaviors that are inappropriate according to the norms of the host culture (Adler, 2002; Francesco & Gold,

2005; Klyukanov, 2005). As a result, they may receive criticism for the behaviors.

The important issue of behavioral style again comes into play (Cingoz-Ulu & Lalonde, 2007). People may be able to accept criticism if it is delivered in a manner that is considered socially skilled in their own culture. However, criticism may be very poorly received if it is offered in an unfamiliar style or in a style that is considered as harsh and uncaring. Problems become especially difficult and hard to diagnose; people offer criticism in a way that they think is socially skilled but that is considered boorish by recipients. Definitions of "socially skilled" and "boorish," of course, depend on the cultural norms where people were socialized.

The impact of disagreements and criticisms are also impacted by disconfirmed expectations. People go on sojourns for a set of positive motives. They want experiences that will expand their worldviews. They want to work on projects that will benefit their career development. They feel that they have resources to offer to people in other countries. So when they have negative experiences brought on by disagreements (Kaushal & Kwantes, 2006) and criticisms, these are acutely felt since they violate the positive expectations people have.

This point can be best communicated by examining experiences in one's own life. Think back on an experience that was negative, which brought up negative emotions, and which caused hurt feelings. In retrospect, was it the experience itself, or was it the distinction between the experience and what was expected. Often, people conclude that the experience was not all that intense. Instead, the negative feelings were brought on because the experience was so different than what people expected.

TAKING DISAGREEMENTS PERSONALLY

To add even more complexity, there are cultural differences in the way people think about themselves and how they think about their opinions (Foa & Chemers, 1967). In some cultures, such as the United States, people make distinctions: there is me as a worthwhile person, and there are my attitudes and opinions concerning a large numbers of social issues. In other cultures, there is not such a distinction. People view themselves and their opinions as part of the same entity. This is the important cultural difference that plays a major role in this incident.

Criticism Taken Personally in Many Cultures

Herb Porter, originally from Seattle, was working in Manila for a company that produced men's and women's business attire. The company had major customers in many large cities throughout Asia, Europe, and North America. Herb had become friendly with Jose Ablaza, given their shared interests in aerobics and weight training. One day, at a meeting attended by about fifteen company employees, Jose presented his ideas for a new marketing plan on which he had been working. Herb made several suggestions that he thought would improve the marketing plan and questioned Jose on one of his assumptions. The next day, Jose did not join Herb at the local gym for their regularly scheduled workout.

There is a possible explanation that I often discuss with North Americans, Pacific Islanders, and Asians who find themselves on overseas assignments. In some cultures, people can disagree with others and still remain on very friendly terms. In other cultures, this combination of behaviors occurs far less frequently. People in these cultures do not make a sharp distinction between "me as a worthwhile individual" and "the ideas I am presenting at this particular meeting." Disagreement with a person's ideas is seen as a challenge to their dignity. The issue of "offering criticism in the workplace" can be a source of strained relationships in many cultures and is frequently covered in cross-cultural training programs.

In this specific case of Herb and Jose, there are culturally appropriate ways for Jose to receive constructive suggestions so that he can improve his marketing plan. Colleagues or bosses who are not close friends can make such suggestions. The people Jose knows can be friends or "constructive critics," but difficulties occur when the same person tries to play both roles. The constructive critics must know culturally appropriate ways of making their suggestions. They would speak one-on-one with Jose after the meeting and would not risk embarrassing him in front of his coworkers. The critics would try to keep the tone of the one-on-one session lighthearted with jokes and pleasant banter. They would make sure that they say good things about the marketing plan and would delicately insert their suggestions for improvement into their positive comments.

If people want to develop the ability to accept disagreement and to remain on friendly terms, my advice is to seek out opportunities for practice. Joining the debate team at school is one good way. Another is to join community organizations and to volunteer for committees where there will surely be disagreements, such as the budget or fund-raising committees.

Challenging the Self-Worth of Others. The importance of the cultural difference involving opinion-self-separation contrasted to opinion-self-integration cannot be overstated. This issue is at the basis of some of the most intense misunderstandings I have observed in thirty-five years of working with sojourners. I was one of the people brought in to help ameliorate the very negative feelings brought on by this incident.

Disagreements Can Threaten Feelings of Self-Worth

"People have been working on marketing plans for about three months, but we'd like to hear your fresh perspectives." Dan Kagawa, born and raised in Hilo, had recently welcomed Krishna Joshi to the marketing division of a digital technology company in Honolulu. Dan knew only a few facts about Krishna's background. He was from New Delhi, India, and was from a prominent and well-respected family. He had attended the prestigious Allahabad University and wanted to develop his entrepreneurial skills by working for a small up-and-coming company in the United States.

Dan had asked Krishna to participate in a staff meeting where the marketing of cellular phones was to be discussed. Krishna shared his view that thirty-second spots on television would be most effective. Kathleen Jacobs disagreed in a direct but pleasant tone of voice. "There are real limitations to a marketing campaign based on television. Cost effectiveness can be a big problem. I feel that we should develop radio spots and place them on stations that will attract drive-time commuters." Other ideas were shared and the meeting was adjourned without a consensus concerning a marketing strategy.

About two days later, Krishna came to Dan's office with a set of complaints. "I can't sleep. I can't eat. I can't face my coworkers in the morning. My entire sense of myself has been attacked." Dan could not figure out why Krishna felt the way he did. Dan reviewed what he knew about Krishna's work and interactions with others, but could not identify a reason for his complaints.

There are several possibilities for Krishna's reactions. In India, he may not have learned to separate disagreements on issues from personal feelings about the disagreements. In many parts of the world, there is a great deal of overlap between "my opinions" and "my feelings about my self-worth." Forthright disagreements, then, can be interpreted as personal attacks. Another possibility is that Krishna is not accustomed to vigorous discussions with women. He may have known women in high school and college, but he may have rarely observed discussions where women argued forcefully about their positions on various issues. A third possibility is that Krishna is more thin-skinned than other professionals from India. If this is the case, then he would have few opportunities to develop a thick skin given his socialization into a prominent Indian family.

The skill of keeping disagreements separate from personal feelings is not easy to develop anywhere in the world. In some cultures, however, people become exposed to this skill as part of school activities such as debate clubs and teachers' assignments to bring in alternative viewpoints for discussions of various social issues. People desirous of improving their skills related to handling disagreements might consider enrolling in evening courses in public speaking or debate offered through college outreach programs.

Familiarity with Arguments and Disagreements. Arguing and bringing up potential areas of disagreement is a common communication style in some cultures (Hammer, 1997). For people in other cultures where arguing is seen as unpleasant and where attempts to find areas of agreement are more common, the argumentative style can be very disturbing.

Arguing Is a Form of Dialogue in Some Cultures

Mark Ozawa, from Honolulu, had traveled to New York City to talk to small businesspeople about the web design company he worked for in Hawaii. He had contacted Abe Rabinowitz, the president of a specialized book publishing company. Mark told Abe that a weekend meeting was possible, adding that he was flexible given that Abe might be attending services at his synagogue.

Mark and Abe met at a restaurant on a Sunday afternoon. When Mark talked about the advantages of working with his company, Abe pointed to the benefits of working with a web design company in New York. When Mark talked about the expanding markets for books in Asia, Abe described horror stories colleagues experienced when they tried to enforce intellectual property rights in China.

After presenting other ideas and hearing opposing arguments, Mark concluded that he and Abe had not found enough common ground that would allow them to do business together.

Abe is using a discussion style that is familiar to Jewish people. The style involves a great deal of argumentation, presentations of disagreements, and exploring multiple aspects of complex issues. The goal of this style is not to win arguments. Rather, the goal is to come as close as possible to discovering and identifying relevant knowledge about complex topics. Jewish adults often remember this style being the basis of family dinner conversations. As teenagers, they would present their thinking, and then parents, aunts, and uncles would take opposing positions. The goal was to put as many issues forward as possible and to explore deeper levels of understanding and meaning.

This argumentative style contributes to excellent preparation for higher education. College students don't take only those courses where they will find ideas with which they already agree. They take courses that expose them to many different positions on complex issues in politics, economics, philosophy, and human behavior. If they are accustomed to discussing various positions based on years of dinner table conversations, they will be well prepared to argue with and to impress professors.

If people want to learn this style, it will likely take a great deal of practice. People should not be discouraged if they enter discussions but find it difficult to argue various sides of issues. They should try again and again and eventually they will become more comfortable. I might add learning to argue in this way has been one of the hardest aspects of my own experiences in intercultural communication.

Many times, people who disagree and offer criticisms do not mean to be harsh and insensitive. They simply are behaving in ways that are familiar in their culture and they want to be helpful. One use of disagreements and criticisms is to put sojourners to the test. If they deal well with the criticisms, they are respected. If they don't, they are dismissed as thin-skinned or unprepared for serious discussions. Sojourners to Australia frequently have stories similar to this one (Mandisodza et al., 2006).

"Tall Poppies" Get Clipped in Australia

"Are you sure that you want me to introduce you by reading this material?" Graham Foster asked his guest, Erin Santos. Graham was the organizer of a workshop in Brisbane, Australia, which had "Seeking Venture Capital" as its theme. Members of the program committee had invited Erin, who was a well-known and successful entrepreneur from Fresno, California. Erin gave Graham a one-page description of herself, hoping to make the task of introducing her easier. The description contained material on honors received in college, awards won as an entrepreneur, and a listing of interviews she had granted to publications such as *Fortune* and *Forbes* magazines.

Graham introduced Erin, and she began her talk. After a few minutes, she was interrupted with questions about the sources of capital for her successful ventures, the originality of her ideas, and the number of years she invested prior to success. One audience member was very direct with a question about why she was flown in from California. "Are you saying that there are no successful entrepreneurs here in Australia?" She tried to answer these questions so that she could continue with her presentation, but at the end of her allotted time she found that she could have spoken for another half-hour.

Erin has encountered the "tall poppy syndrome." When I ask Australian businesspeople about cultural difference that visitors might observe, this is the example they most frequently report. Tall poppies refer to high status people who might be challenged and "chopped down" so that they fall from their lofty perches. In Erin's case, she was frequently challenged about how she had obtained her status. Did she have a clear business plan to attract investors, or did she just take advantage of family money? Did she have good ideas herself, or did she benefit from others' innovations?

She was a tall poppy being challenged, and she had to defend her accomplishments that led to the invitation from the conference organizers. Australians are much less inclined to cut down tall poppies if they are seen as deserving their high status.

Norman Feather (2003) points out that the tall poppy syndrome serves the Australian value of social equality. People should not put themselves above others. When challenged, people should be modest about their accomplishments, give credit to others who have helped, and they should communicate with graciousness and a sense of humor. For Americans, communicating in this manner can be practiced before traveling to Australia.

GOALS SERVED BY DISAGREEMENTS AND CRITICISMS

As has been discussed several times, communication serves people's goals. Some of the goals are found in many countries. Criticisms can have the purpose of improvement. Disagreements can serve the goal of putting many ideas on the table so that people have many alternatives to discuss (Janis, 1982). There are also culturally specific reasons, as we have seen in the example of tall poppies in Australia. In Germany, people engage in very intense discussions so that they will avoid hearing the criticism that they are unaware of current and historical events.

Expecting Intense Discussions about Political Issues

Knowing that his German colleagues will likely expect him to participate in discussions on political issues, Jim Foley made a point of reading the *Washington Post* and the *New York Times* over a six-month period. Jim was from Richmond, Virginia, and had worked as an engineer in several American firms over the last ten years. He accepted a position with the consumer electronics division of Siemens in Bonn, Germany. Since he had projects in the United States to complete, he asked for and was granted a full year between signing a contract with Siemens and actually moving to Germany.

Jim's initial interactions with his German colleagues went well, but after a time he found that he could not keep up with the intensity of discussions about political matters. These issues would be discussed during work breaks, after-hours gatherings at beer halls, and at social events during weekends. He found that he could follow arguments regarding current government policies on issues such as the treatment of Turkish guest workers. However, he could not contribute to discussions when German colleagues brought in insights from their reading of European history, philosophy, and sociology.

One reason for intense discussions about politics and government is that Germans born after World War II do not want events of the twentieth century repeated. Many have asked their townspeople, including their parents, about the Third Reich. "What did you know at the time? Were you aware of the Holocaust? What was your relation to the Nazi Party?" Many Germans say that they received vague answers to these questions, such as, "We may have had suspicions but we weren't sure." To prevent the repetition of the past, Germans today expect each other to be well informed and to keep up with complex discussions that demand extensive knowledge. They have agreed that they will never be able to use the excuse, "We didn't know." Referring to this century's history, they sometimes use the phrase, "Nie wieder," or "Never again."

Visitors to Germany often point out that there are many artifacts in Germany that provide constant reminders of World War II. These include concentration camps that tourists visit, books in every department store, and monuments in every town. Germans today agree that their discussion style can be uncomfortable for some people, but it is preferable to the ignorance that allows evil to go unchallenged.

For any piece of general advice that people might offer to sojourners, there will be interesting exceptions. In some cultures, people actively seek out criticism. They want to improve themselves, and they identify successful and prominent individuals who might offer constructive advice. This practice is probably more common in cultures that have strong hierarchies and where authority figures receive a great deal of deference. But if the people from whom criticism is sought are unfamiliar with this cultural difference, they can become very uncomfortable.

Self Cultivation and the Question, "How Can I Improve?"

"This should be an uneventful meeting," Leonard Farr said to himself as he reviewed the progress report prepared by Fumio Ogawa. Leonard was director of research and development at a pharmaceutical company near Cleveland, Ohio. Fumio, originally from Chiba, Japan, was a biochemist working on drugs to treat liver cancer. Fumio had great respect for Leonard and considered him a role model. Leonard had won prizes and had been awarded patents for his earlier work on treatments for diabetes.

Leonard greeted Fumio, closed the office door, and started his yearly performance evaluation. He pointed out that Fumio was a hard worker, was creative in his thinking, kept clear and detailed laboratory notes, and was on track to be promoted in about a year. Fumio replied, "Thank you, but please tell me what I have not been doing well and what I can do to improve." Leonard was not prepared for a question this direct concerning areas for improvement.

In Japan, there is a value placed on self-improvement and self-cultivation so that an individual becomes a better person. A commonly used term in Japanese is "hansei," and it refers to reflecting on one's short-coming and investing effort into improving oneself. One way to discover ways of improving is to seek out feedback from superiors in the work-place. To further the goals of hansei, negative information is far more diagnostic than positive feedback. People learn more about how to improve if they hear, "Your public speaking style is a little bit dull" than if they hear a litany of workplace behaviors that they do well.

As with many workplace behaviors, details of the social context in which a cultural difference might occur have to be understood (Richardson & Smith, 2007). Fumio might not ask his question of just anybody. He would ask for ways to improve only from people he respects a great deal, as in this incident with Leonard. Fumio may feel that he has a very good relationship with his boss that is strong enough to withstand a yearly performance review that contains some negative feedback. In addition, Fumio is likely to seek this feedback only in one-on-one meetings behind closed doors. Negative feedback would not be welcome in a public forum since Fumio might loose face (Shigemasu & Ikeda, 2006) in front of his peers.

To work effectively with Japanese and others Asians (e.g., Koreans, Chinese), Leonard should prepare himself for direct inquiries concerning how subordinates can improve themselves. The tone of voice and vocabulary he uses can be gentle. Throughout their socialization, Japanese learn to be careful listeners and learn to benefit from gently placed suggestions concerning self-development.

Working through Disagreements. There are other ways of dealing with workplaces where people hold very differing opinions. Some individuals are good at working with people who disagree intensely and who are all too willing to offer criticism to those who disagree with them. These individuals are sometimes called workplace politicians, and here I am using the term politician in the best sense (Crick, 1982). Good politicians can listen to people with different viewpoints, show respect, and develop compromise positions with which people on opposite sides of issues can agree.

Office Politicians Can Be An Important Asset

With her double major in public relations and marketing, Masako Horoiwa interviewed well and was offered a job at the convention center in Providence, Rhode Island. Originally from Tokyo, she had attended Michigan State University under an international exchange of scholars program. She thought that her job prospects in the United States would be better than in Japan, and she was pleased when she was offered the convention center position. After a few weeks at work, she had lunch with her supervisor, Steve Hudson. A colleague, Grace Morris, came by their table for a short chat. After she left, Steve said, "Grace is a good office politician. If you can get to know her I think it will benefit both of you." Having read of recent ethics investigations of politicians in both Tokyo and Providence, Masako was unclear about Steve's use of the term, "office politician."

Good office politicians are important assets in the workplace. They have good networks both inside and outside the organization. A marketing manager, for instance, will know accountants, human resource specialists, and financial officers, all of whom can offer various forms of help on important projects. Good office politicians will also know people outside the organization, such as lawyers, professors, and physicians. In marketing conventions, for example, it is very useful to know lots of professionals who can mention a specific convention city to their associations' conference planners.

Good politicians can form alliances among people who do not care for each other and who do not normally communicate with each other. They can identify issues on which people might agree and choose not to spend time on multiple areas of disagreement. They can identify issues on which people can say, "It will be more useful to collaborate with members of this other group than to ignore them." This means that politicians are good at communicating answers to the question, "What's in it for me?" when they talk to various groups whose members are often at odds with each other.

These activities assure that they will be in the presence of people who will shout at each other during the time necessary to thrash out differences and to identify areas of possible collaboration. Good politicians remain calm, listen carefully to all points of view, and are models of pleasantness and cooperation. Most people have attended meetings where opinions are voiced loudly and with a harsh tone of voice. Who communicates effectiveness and political skillfulness? Is it the shouters, or is it the people who remain calm and collected? When people remain calm, they can focus their energies on identifying issues around which coalitions might be formed.

7

Decision Making

THE RATIONAL MODEL

Good decision making is central to the work of managers and to the development and maintenance of effective workplaces (Gupta & Govindarajan, 2000). Most of the examples in this chapter will involve decision making by managers when they are on international assignments. When making decisions, managers can rely on their gut instincts, remember the advice of the last person with whom they spoke, or they can engage in a more formal process. In the rational decision-making model, managers first ask, "What are the goals of this decision-making process?" They then gather relevant information, being careful to assess its reliability. Then, they list criteria related to the decision. After this step, they place weights on the criteria depending on importance and centrality to an eventual good decision. Finally, they compare various alternative possibilities to the weighted criteria. The alternative consistent with the largest number of weighted criteria becomes the decision that the managers make.

This formal process becomes clearer with a specific example. Managers need to make decisions concerning whom to hire. They gather various types of information, including the workloads of current employees, projected expansions of products and services, the nature of the current job market, and the salary offers needed to attract good applicants. They then list the criteria of people who will make good employees. These criteria can include public speaking ability, writing skills, experience in leadership positions, a background of successful project completion, experience working as members of teams, information processing skills, and specific knowledge necessary for work success. Then, these criteria are weighted. If the job calls for a great deal of face-to-face interaction with potential customers, oral presentation skills may be weighted higher than writing skills. If the job calls for frequent interaction with others on complex projects, experience working with teams may be weighted higher than information processing skills.

After the criteria are given weights, advertisements for job openings can be posted. After various applications and resumes are gathered, the qualifications of various candidates can be compared to the criteria. Decision-makers then develop ratings based on comparisons of criteria to qualifications. These ratings can take the form of numbers indicating how well qualifications match the criteria, or they can be summarized as a simple rank ordering of candidates from highest to lowest. The candidates who score highest on the most criteria can then be invited for interviews. After talking with the candidates, the decision-makers can examine their original ratings and make adjustments based on information and impressions gathered during the interviews. The candidate with the highest score then receives a job offer.

In my experience, different decision-makers find reasons for disagreements at any time during the process. Disagreements about criteria and weights are especially interesting since they reflect differences in the backgrounds of managers. In collective societies where group ties are extremely important, there may be criteria such as family ties to people already in the organization or shared experiences at the same high school as current employees. In societies where hierarchy is important and where leaders do the talking and newly hired subordinates do the listening, there may not be a large weight placed on public speaking skills. In hierarchical societies, decision-makers might also add a criterion that deals with the prestige of the school that applicants attended (Triandis, 1995). In these societies, the relative prestige of schools is widely known, and parents place great emphasis on getting their children into "the right schools."

Many decisions are made that do not follow this rational model. Rather, people make decisions based on information that comes quickly to mind or that appeals to their emotions. In addition, people simply do not have enough time to go through the rational process for every decision they must make. Good managers learn to make the distinction between important decisions that demand the rational process and less important decisions that can be made much more quickly.

Placing Different Weights on Decision Criteria. In this incident, two people agree on the goals of the hiring process. They want to hire people who will contribute to the future of their company. But they disagree on the weights attached to different criteria, and their weighting reflects their cultural background.

Cultural Expectations: Lockstep and Flexible Schedules

Knowing that future plans called for more expansion into North American markets, the divisional director of Samsung Electronics wanted to hire two entry-level managers with good English language skills. He asked Minho Lee and Phil Harris to review applications, conduct interviews, and to make recommendations. Minho was a Korean national and Phil was an American who had lived in Korea for eight years.

Minho was impressed with the application of Junkee Park, who was twenty-six years old. Junkee had attended Yonsei University where he took as many English courses as possible, and he had also completed three years of military service. Phil preferred Bob Evans, originally from Phoenix, Arizona, who was thirty-two years old. Bob had traveled for two years after high school graduation, then went to a community college, and then worked for a construction company. After completing his bachelor's degree, he accepted a position teaching English in Korea. Even though Minho and Phil recommended that both candidates be hired, they were puzzled with each other's level of enthusiasm for their favorite candidate.

The cultural difference is based on expectations of what good job candidates should bring to an interview. In Korea, candidates are impressive if their behavior has been "lockstep." They go to high school, start college when eighteen years old, have three years of military service, and then present themselves to the job market at age twenty-five or twenty-six. If they deviate from this lockstep pattern, they may send the message that they are not serious and hardworking people. In the United States, expectations about job candidates are more open. People can take a few years off from formal schooling, can obtain work experience, and can develop skills hard to acquire in the classroom. These candidates often communicate desirable qualities such as creativity, independence, and willingness to take risks. Community colleges, in which people can enroll anytime during their adulthood, allow people to move away from lockstep expectations concerning age and formal education.

The lockstep system may be changing slowly. One of the first challenges occurred with Koreans who traveled to North America for a year of intense English language instruction. This was frowned upon ten years ago but is now much more common and is even encouraged by Korean companies interested in candidates with language skills.

Some cultural misunderstandings occur because one of the parties in the intercultural decision-making process is unaware of some of the criteria. One person has a perfectly sensible set of criteria from his or her point of view, and the other person also has sensible criteria from the same personal viewpoint. But there may be no or minimal overlap in one or more of the criteria, and people may be unaware of this fact. In this incident, one of the people involved had a task in mind: deciding whether or not to spend a year in another country. The other person had a social goal in mind: making sure that people have good interpersonal relationships.

Decision Making: Task and Social Goals

Dallas resident Don White worked for a small financial planning firm. Winai Kitjaroen, from Thailand, worked for a large investment firm in Bangkok. They met at a workshop dealing with Asian capital markets held in Hong Kong. Don and Winai found they shared both professional and personal interests and spent much of their free time together. Don mentioned that his firm allows employees to spend up to a year in other countries as part of its international expansion goals. Winai replied, "It would be nice if you could come to Bangkok. I'll tell my executives about your interest." Don returned to Dallas and received e-mails from Winai, but there was never any mention of an invitation to spend a year in Bangkok.

Negotiations about important issues such as a yearlong overseas assignment will be based on many factors including cultural issues, the personalities of people, and changing organizational priorities. One cultural difference starts with the fact that there are at least two goals in communications among businesspeople. One is social: people want to make others feel good about the social interactions they are having. Another goal deals with tasks: people want to make plans that will improve the financial performance of their organizations. In Thailand and in other Asian cultures, the social goals can take precedence. Winai wants a good relationship with Don and so makes a positive comment about a year in Thailand. Don is concerned with tasks since he needs time to plan for a year in Thailand.

Experienced sojourners familiar with this cultural difference would advise Bob to probe for specific details concerning the one-year assignment. What would be the scope of jointly agreed upon projects? In addition to Winai, who else would be working with me? How much secretarial help will be available? If there are not answers to specific inquiries, this could be a sign that the assignment has become low priority in Winai's organization.

Many cultural differences can be better understood if similar dilemmas are identified in a person's own country. Bob has surely been to evening receptions where he meets someone who later says, "Let's have lunch." Was this a pleasant comment to keep positive conversations going, or was it a sincere invitation? Like all of us who have encountered this comment, we face difficulties deciding whether to call for a lunch appointment or not.

Obtaining Information Necessary for Decision Making. Part of the decision-making process involves obtaining as much information and as many suggestions as possible. In some cultures, managers assign people to do research so as to obtain as many facts as possible relevant to the upcoming decision. Then, people come together and share information and suggest possible alternatives, one or more of which will eventually be chosen as the decision that will direct future action. A common approach to making suggestions in some cultures is to engage in brainstorming, but this is not an accepted method in all cultures. Managers need to know how alternatives are formulated and how one or more is chosen, as in this example.

Decision Making: Taking Care of the Roots

"Tokyo is beautiful when the cherry blossoms are in full bloom," Peter Nolan said to himself as he entered the Honda Motors office building. "I wish I had the same positive feelings about last week's meeting attended by company executives." Peter was from Cleveland, Ohio, and had two degrees in mechanical engineering. He worked for an automobile parts manufacturer and had been given an assignment to develop markets in Asian-owned factories. He contacted various Honda plants in Ohio and Indiana and eventually was invited to company headquarters in Japan.

Peter was introduced at one of the company's biweekly meetings and was asked to say a few words about himself. He took this opportunity to talk about his marketing goals and to present his thinking about combining the best of American and Japanese management practices in the automobile industry. He thought that there would be a few encouraging comments or some insightful questions, but his presentation was met with a chilly silence. Secretaries later told him that various company executives had become unavailable for previously scheduled meetings.

There are well-established norms in Japan for making business decisions, and Peter broke them. At meetings in the United States, people can bring up issues that have previously not been discussed and they can expect open discussions. This is part of the decision-making process called brainstorming. In Japan, a person who wants to introduce an issue needs to discuss it with others in various one-on-one meetings. These are held behind closed doors and are scheduled at the convenience of Japanese managers and executives. Objections and suggestions for improvement are shared and dealt with in these meetings. Much later, the decision may be announced at an open meeting that is more a ceremony than an opportunity for further discussion. The danger of bringing up new issues in open meetings is that someone may feel unprepared to make appropriate comments. They might become embarrassed in front of their Japanese colleagues, and this is an emotion they want to avoid.

The Japanese term for this decision-making style is "nemawashi." The term is an adaptation from an agricultural practice where farmers are very careful about the roots of trees that are transplanted from one place to another. Applied to the business world, people who might be involved in decision making or implementation are "roots," and these must be given special care and attention.

DECISION MAKING IN CHINESE BUSINESSES

In many collective societies, trust among individuals takes a long time to develop. Membership in collectives involves many obligations and also the right to draw from the resources of others in the collective. Given the centrality of people's collectives to their work and personal lives, membership is not offered lightly. The exception is family membership. People automatically become part of a family collective the moment they are born. People are socialized in such a collective to be proud of their family name, to work hard so that they can make contributions to the family, and to work cooperatively with relatives. Given that people put so much time and energy into their family collectives, they often do not have many opportunities to develop trusting relationships with outsiders. Consequently, if the family is the center of a business, relatives are likely to be favored over outsiders who happen to be hired into a family business.

This favoritism shown toward family members can be seen in Chinese family businesses. Chinese businesses provide an especially interesting case since they have been successful all over the world (Kelley & Luo, 1999; Ng & Roberts, 2007). The manner in which Chinese family businesses run can be very surprising to businesspeople familiar with (what they think is) rational decision making.

Differing Views of Entrepreneurship among Chinese Businesspeople

"Entrepreneurship in Asia! Sounds interesting," Ann Nelson said to herself as she examined an invitation from the Advanced Management Institute in Bangkok, Thailand. Working out of Hong Kong for the last four years, Ann had started a small export business and had also invested in an old friend's textile company. Ann and her friend had been high school classmates in Detroit and had been active in the Junior Achievement program. Her successful business was featured in an article in the *Asian Wall Street Journal*, and this was the basis of her invitation to the conference in Bangkok.

Ann was asked to give a talk on American entrepreneurship. She did so early in the program, and it seemed to be well received. However, when other participants gave their talks, they seemed to be speaking another language even though all presentations were in English. Ann seemed especially confused when Chinese businesspeople from Singapore, Malaysia, and Thailand spoke. They described successful businesses, but the steps they took to be successful were alien to Ann's experiences. Ann felt like a character in *Alice in Wonderland*, trying to figure out what was going on during this topsy-turvy conference.

When Americans and offshore Chinese speak about entrepreneurship, they have different models in mind. In America, the model includes steps such as researching consumer needs and demands, identifying underdeveloped niches, preparing a careful business plan, attracting an initial set of investors, later approaching venture capitalists, and possibly proposing an initial public offering. Among Chinese businesspeople, models of entrepreneurship start with the family. Family members work together in a small business. Hardworking young family members are identified. Some may start their own businesses with investments from parents, uncles, and cousins. Many times, the businesses are integrated. For example, if the initial business was a restaurant, the new entrepreneurial venture could be a company supplying plates, silverware, and linen.

As part of their obligations as good members of a collective, uncles and older cousins are expected to invest in various businesses controlled by family members. Profits are plowed back into business expansion or are invested in real estate. If entrepreneurs fail with their first ventures, family members often will support a second attempt, but that is the limit. After two failed attempts, elders will find a place in an existing family business for a person who has not demonstrated entrepreneurial skills. Sons and daughters in their early teens learn the principles of business by working for the family, an asset known as "sweat equity." Men from outside the family who are courting daughters will be looked upon more favorably if they bring assets that can be used in family businesses.

The Experiences of Outsiders. When Chinese businesses are successful and find that they must expand, there are two possible routes. One is to break a large business into two or more entities, each part run by a relative. Another route is to hire people from outside the family. This can cause frustration for well-educated and able nonfamily members.

Non-Family Members and Chinese Family Businesses

After three years of seventy-hour weeks, Xiaojing Liu felt that she was ready for a promotion. Xiaojing had been hired by a family owned business in Taipei, Taiwan. Not a family member herself, she had received an MBA from an American university and was hired because of her expertise in accounting and information technology systems. The family business produced high-end women fashions that were sold at upscale boutiques in cities around the world. Xiaojing applied for a position that would have substantially increased her salary. Instead, the position went to the niece of the company president. "I know that I shouldn't be surprised," Xiaojing told a friend. "But it still stings after all the contributions I have made to the company."

Xiaojing is facing problems encountered by many "outsiders" who work for Chinese family businesses. On the one hand, they are part of the company and often can become quite close to its executives. On the other hand, there are people whose family ties make them closer to executives: sons, daughters, nephews, nieces, and cousins. Nonfamily members are confronted by many difficult decisions. They constantly debate whether to tell the truth about company performance, or to tell what the family members want to hear. At times, nonfamily members have a difficult time knowing how the company is doing. Financial information is often tightly controlled by the family. If the information would embarrass a family member, it is even more likely to remain unreleased. Nonfamily members wonder why some people were hired. It often seems that people are in certain positions because of their kinship connections instead of their capabilities.

Executives face pressures when making promotion decisions. If they promote outsiders such as Xiaojing, they must be prepared to explain their decisions to irate family members. They must deal with comments such as, "You didn't choose your niece! Don't you remember that she has worked for the company since she was fourteen years old and still going to school full time? What sort of message are you sending to other family members who have shown such loyalty to the company?"

In my interviews with outsiders hired into Chinese family businesses (Wang, Brislin, Wang, Williams, & Chao, 2000), some employees balance reports of their negative experiences with more positive features of their work. Family businesses control a large portion of the world's wealth, so they must be carefully analyzed and understood rather than dismissed as hotbeds of nepotism. Family ownership contributes to the stability of businesses over multiple generations. If people can accept the downsides, company executives take good care of employees whom they learn to trust and value.

Marrying into the Family. Two routes for business expansion have been discussed: splitting one large company into two or more, with each part run by a family member, and hiring nonfamily members. A third route is to offer mentoring to able people who marry into Chinese families. This process can be very complex and can entail incredible stress for people not prepared for the many expectations that the status of "in-law" entails.

Daughters, Sons-in-Law, and Chinese Family Businesses

"Are you sure you know what you are getting into?" Kevin Suzuki asked Dan Chung. "My knowledge of Chinese family businesses is mostly from books, but I have read that sons-in-law often have a difficult time." Kevin and Dan, both from Honolulu, were roommates during their college years and developed a very close relationship where all topics could be discussed. Dan had just told Kevin that he was thinking of asking Wong Mei to marry him. Dan had worked for Wong Mei's father in Taipei, Taiwan, for the last five years. The business was family owned, and Wong Mei was a respected manager.

Kevin knew that Wong Mei had sisters but no brothers. He wondered what the father, Wong Lung, would do when it came time to choose a successor. If Wong Lung behaved according to traditional norms, he would take a series of steps. After the marriage, Dan would change his name so that the Wong family line could continue. With a strong preference that sons inherit the family business, Dan would become the owner and president of the company. If Dan and Wong Mei had a son, Dan would be expected to groom him to become the company president. This would mean that the son would have few choices about making his own life decisions, and Dan might eventually become uncomfortable imposing these expectations.

Dan is likely to face other difficulties. He will be seen as an outsider and there will always be the feeling among many that he married Wong Mei for her money. Wong Mei had been a respected manager, and there will be some who feel that she should have inherited the company. Wong Lung may be a traditionalist, but this does not mean that all people in the company agree with him regarding the preference that sons receive inheritances. Many people in the company may feel that Wong Lung's preferences are archaic and that talented daughters should be allowed to rise to the top of the organization.

There are other problems that might occur in a marriage between Dan and Wong Mei. If Wong Mei disagrees with how Dan is running the company, she can intervene by forming coalitions with relatives. Wong Mei will likely win given her lifelong relations with extended family members. Dan might become a figurehead who has to have major decisions approved by his wife. Harmony at home may become dependent upon Dan's acceptance of Wong Mei's directives concerning the family business.

HEURISTICS AND DECISION MAKING

Use of rational decision models is not always possible. People are very busy and face many decisions on a daily basis. In the business world, these include decisions about workplace improvements, service to customers, contributions to the campaigns of political candidates, expansion of markets into other countries, recommendations for employee involvement in voluntary community service projects, and so forth. In a perfect world, people would have infinite time to make decisions about these issues. They would have the time and energy to research the issues, list pros and cons of many possible choices, and apply weights to various options corresponding to their importance. With all this information, they would be able to make careful, highly rational decisions. But the world is not perfect. People simply do not have enough time for this type of careful decision making.

Instead, people rely on heuristics. These guidelines to quick if imperfect decision making are also known as "rules of thumb." Heuristics often can be summarized in memorable phrases or images that come quickly to mind. People then recall these phrases and images when it comes time to make a decision. Instead of reading every review before going out to a movie, a person can say, "Roger Ebert gave it three stars." Instead of studying every make and model before purchasing an automobile, a person can remember the advertisements that featured several enthusiastic buyers talking about the respect they received at a certain dealership. Instead of considering all options for entertainment at a preschooler's birthday party, a person can remember the heuristic that kids always like clowns who can make balloon animals.

I have used various heuristics in this book to communicate material about cultural differences and to help people make good decisions during their intercultural interactions. I have pointed out that there is often a home field advantage when deciding how to behave in the face of cultural differences. One critical incident dealt with the heuristic that tall poppies are likely to be cut down in Australia. In many collective cultures, children learn that the heuristic "silence is golden" serves the goal of preserving harmony within groups.

Some quick guides to decision making are called availability heuristics because they come quickly to mind. If people are contemplating buying a car and the thought comes to mind that they should check *Consumer*

Reports or *Car and Driver* for independent ratings, then they are behaving according to the availability heuristic.

Heuristics sometimes take the form of problems that have recently occurred, caused stress and upheaval, and that people do not want to see repeated. The desire to avoid a recent problem is central to this critical incident.

Recent Events Overshadow Record

In a small company in Hawaii (200 employees), people have long experienced very cordial relations with each other and they frequently have socialized outside the workplace. In the last fifteen years, there has not been a major problem involving personnel. Reimbursement for travel expenses and claims for overtime pay were processed on an informal basis and on an honor system. But recently, it was discovered that one of the employees had been embezzling money for the last two years. The president of the company established a strict set of policies for the processing of employee expense accounts, purchases from outside vendors, and the paperwork for sick leave and annual leave. Employees began to complain among themselves that they were no longer trusted and they had to complete so much paperwork that they had far less time for their actual job assignments.

One reason for the president's decision to make changes is that people pay a great deal of attention to recent colorful events. They give less attention to combining information from the new events with information from the past. In this case, the president bases decisions on the recent negative event and does not consider it just one piece of information to be combined with the positive experiences of the last fifteen years. The president's decision can be especially controversial in Hawaii since many people enjoy workplaces with informal rather than strict rules for conduct.

Attention to recent events helps explain many decisions that people make. We might be at the airport to welcome a friend, and a flight from Las Vegas arrives as we wait. The person who "won big" at the slot machines is welcomed by members of his extended family. Do we carefully think about the majority of people who have lost money in Las Vegas, or is our attention directed at the excitement surrounding this big winner? People who consider running for political office are taught this aspect of human behavior in seminars. Experienced politicians tell a joke that they frequently share among themselves. A politician is running for her eighth two-years term. Talking with a constituent, she reminds him of the help she gave ten, seven, six, and three years ago. For instance, she reminds him that seven years ago, she spoke up for his nephew when he sought his first job after college. "Yes, but what have you done for me recently?" the constituent asks.

Realizing that people's attention is drawn to recent events that will be fresh in their memories, politicians often work on popular legislative actions during the months prior to their reelection campaigns. In so doing, they are taking advantage of an availability heuristic since recent actions are likely to pop quickly to mind as voters read over a slate of candidates.

Adages Can Guide Decision Making. Some heuristics are summarized by adages that become part of the commonly shared language in a culture. As a child I learned "A stitch in time saves nine" as a reminder to prevent big problems tomorrow by taking small preventive steps today. I learned the adage, "People in glass houses shouldn't throw stones," and this has come to mind when I have been tempted to criticize others. In this incident, an American encounters a Chinese heuristic while working in Shanghai.

Waiting for the Golden Moment to Introduce New Ideas

With four years of college-level Chinese that included a summer immersion program, Tom Saunders had little difficulty communicating with coworkers in Shanghai. Tom had been hired as an information technology specialist at a large import-export business. He worked closely with Zhang Lei, who oversaw marketing efforts in the United States and Europe. Tom knew that Zhang wanted to introduce a new marketing campaign based on printed ads placed in specialized trade journals. Zhang mentioned to Tom that he would be recommending the campaign to his boss, Hai Qiang. Tom said, "I think you should do it as soon as possible. I can help with technical information that could be integrated into the ads." But Zhang did not move as fast as Tom desired.

Zhang may be waiting for "the golden moment." In China, this is a frequently heard term and it refers to the best time to introduce an innovation or any change in the status quo. Zhang may be waiting for a sign from Hai Qiang that he is ready to hear about innovative proposals. Or, Zhang may be waiting until his boss makes decisions on other pressing issues and so has time to give full attention to new proposals. Or, Zhang may know that Hai Qiang is very careful to keep abreast of what major competitors are doing. If the competition makes changes in its approaches to marketing, Zhang may know that this is the "golden moment" to approach his boss.

Golden moments are chosen for many behaviors. A man and woman may have been dating for several years, but they may wait for a good time to discuss their engagement with their parents. At times, specialists are consulted who have reputations for being able to predict the future. These specialists gather background information and then make recommendations for the best days to carry out certain activities, such as a job search or move to a new home.

Waiting for the golden moment becomes part of social skills in China. To maintain the harmony called for in a collectivistic culture, people become very sensitive to each other's moods and preferences. If decision-makers are busy, or are having personal problems that makes concentration on work difficult, then socially sensitive individuals will wait for a better time to approach their bosses. When people work with others for a long time, they learn to read very subtle cues concerning whether a boss is approachable or not. Given that Tom is a relative newcomer to the organization, he has probably not had the opportunity to observe people over a long period of time. He may not pick up on social cues that are quite obvious to Zhang Lei.

8

Interactions among Males and Females

INTRODUCTION: GENDER ROLES AND CHANGE

About twenty years ago, I was in a conversation about research with a much younger colleague. He was planning a longitudinal study of worker behavior in different cultures and asked me for advice. He wanted to investigate a workplace issue that would certainly change in the future. He planned to measure attitudes and behaviors at one point in time, and then to measure them again in about thirty years. My suggestion was to investigate the contributions of, and interactions among, males and females in the workplace.

My suggestion was based on various pieces of information that were widely available twenty years ago and are still descriptive of behavior in the workplace. In many countries, more and more women are seeking higher education and are then applying for jobs in corporations (Adler, 2002; Hung, Li, & Belk, 2007). Workplace restrictions on certain types of interactions among men and women, more commonly called sexual harassment prevention guidelines, have been developed. Women are refusing to accept traditional workplace norms such as accepting the status of receptionists and office assistants and then quitting work when they get married. In many parts of the world (Japan, France, Italy), women are putting off marriage and, once married, are having so few children that demographers are predicting that there will be population decreases since there will be fewer births than deaths. Given that women are putting off marriage, the workplace is likely to be a place where male–female pairings into romantic unions start. If women do not begin to think about marriage until age thirty or more, schools will decline in prominence as the answer to the question, "Where did you meet?"

These observations and others make male–female interactions an important topic for study. Complexity is added in intercultural interactions since people learn norms for male–female interactions during their socialization in one culture. They then bring these norms to their interactions during their sojourns in other countries. Sometimes their familiar and well-learned behaviors will be well received, and sometimes they will break social norms.

THE UNDERLYING REASONS FOR MALE–FEMALE DIFFERENCES

Whenever we encounter misunderstandings, we should look to possible underlying reasons. Various types of writings are filled with examples of male–female miscommunications. Descriptions can be found in oral tradition (e.g., Ulysses and Penelope), written literature (*Romeo and Juliet*), in news stories (Judge Clarence Thomas and Anita Hill), and in the scholarly journals of such fields as psychology, communication, anthropology, and sociology. Males and females often bring different perspectives to their communications. Two major classes of reasons have been suggested, and both will be covered in the discussions of different critical incidents. One class of reasons involves biological differences (Buss, 2000). Women and men have different roles in the procreation and rearing of children. This leads to obvious physical differences, such as breasts for feeding, but also to psychological differences in approaches to mating. Women have to be more careful, or in everyday language, more picky. For women, a sex act (especially before today's knowledge of contraception) could lead to a nine-month pregnancy and years of child rearing. For men, a sex act does not have such implications unless they have deeply committed relationships with women whom they have impregnated. And so we return to carefulness and pickiness. Women want to be sure that the men with whom they perform sex acts will not disappear if they conceive.

One aspect of the fact that women conceive children and men do not is especially interesting because it has implications for workplace interactions. Our biology is shaped by our evolutionary past. One of the basic assumptions in evolutionary theory is that our distant ancestors behaved in ways that increased the chances of their survival. If certain behaviors led to survival, then they became well established and passed on from generation to generation. Some of these behaviors became so privileged that people's brains developed to make their acquisition possible. Examples are language learning, the startle reflex when there is danger nearby, and the ability to form alliances with others. Another example, with implications for today's workplaces, is the interaction of males and females.

For humans to survive into future generations, they must mate and have children. Men and women look for different features in potential mates. Men look for youth and physical attractiveness. Youth is central since there are limits to the child-bearing years of women. Attractiveness is a sign that women are healthy, and so babies they bear may also be healthy. Women are looking for men with status and resources. They need men able to provide resources and during the years necessary to raise children until they become self-sufficient. Men with high status titles and resources that can be exchanged for food and shelter are desirable.

In today's world, remnants of this age-old exchange of youth and attractiveness lead to frequently seen behaviors. Women dress and make themselves up to be attractive to members of the opposite sex. Men learn to present themselves in ways that emphasize their status and earnings potential. They may drive expensive cars, for example, to persuade women that they have a great deal of money. Some behaviors border on the inappropriate. Imagine a social gathering at the office that takes place at 5:00 P.M. on a Friday. The purpose of the gathering is to welcome the new company vice president. There are about 100 people present, some of them young and attractive and others who are older and well established in their careers. Who will, perhaps inappropriately, focus their attentions on young and attractive people so that they can improve their social lives?

Men are more likely than women to turn the gathering into opportunities for dating.

Who will focus their attentions on older and well-established people who might have favors to distribute? Women are more likely to turn the gathering into opportunities to increase their resources in the forms of improved professional networks, information about promotions, and the development of political alliances in the workplace. This quest for favors is one reason older executives learn to dislike company parties. They complain that they came to have a good time, but all that happens is that they are hustled for favors.

These tendencies are subject to cultural changes (Hofstede, 2001; House et al., 2004). Given recent workplace policies concerning sexual harassment, men have to be careful about their interactions with females. And given that women can now earn large salaries and can hold down high status jobs, they do not always need to be dependent upon men for resources.

The fact that there can be cultural change over years introduces us to the other class of reasons for male–female differences: social learning (Cross & Gore, 2003). People learn various roles and behaviors appropriate for males and females as part of their socialization. Females learn when they can interact with males, and males with females, without being considered deviant. They learn what jobs are traditionally open to males and females. They learn norms such as appropriate ages for marriage, whether marriage partners are based on self-selection or are arranged by parents, and they learn whether divorce is socially acceptable or not.

There is no necessary contradiction between biological and social learning viewpoints. Knowledge of biology can provide a starting point (e.g., labor during birth weakens women and so they need resources provided by others), but social learning can provide a rich overlay of details (who provides the resources, what exactly are the resources, are there ceremonies attached to the presentation of the resources?). While I will occasionally touch on biological explanations (I have covered these in more detail in Brislin, 2000), I will be emphasizing social learning explanations in this chapter since successful intercultural communication demands knowledge of the rich overlay of cultural norms surrounding male–female interactions. And, I believe, sojourners are more likely to need social learning explanations for intercultural misunderstandings than they are likely to need biological explanations.

Acceptable Behaviors for Men and Women

As has been discussed several times, norms refer to socially acceptable standards of behavior. All cultures develop norms for what is appropriate for men and what is appropriate for women. A major cultural difference involves the *relative amount* of distinctiveness between behaviors considered appropriate for men and women (Hofstede, 2001). In some cultures, the distinctiveness is strikingly large. In other cultures, the distinctiveness is much less.

What Do Men and Women Do in Different Countries?

After just three months in Stockholm, Sweden, Steve Fisher noticed many aspects of work and social interactions that differed from his previous experiences in Tallahassee, Florida. Steve had accepted a managerial job with a Swedish pharmaceutical company that was planning expansions into North American markets. Steve was single, twenty-seven years old, and was picking up conversational Swedish quickly.

Steve observed that there were many female bosses. Reading the newspaper, he also discovered that there were large number of female government officials. He met women whose husbands stayed home and raised the children. When a woman was about to give birth, he heard about government programs for both maternity and paternity leave. After meeting single women in the workplace, some seemed very comfortable asking him out to dinner and to theatrical presentations. From friends, he heard that women often propose marriage rather than wait for men they have been dating to take the lead.

The differences Steve observed follow from cultural guidelines summarized by the term, "low gender differentiation." The best way to understand this term is to start with the question, "What do men do and what do women do in this country?" Beyond biological facts surrounding procreation, cultures with low gender differentiation have few distinctions to mark what women can do and what men can do. In high gender differentiation cultures, there are many distinctions that have a long tradition. For example, men are the bosses and women are the secretaries. Men go to work and women stay home and raise children. Men take the lead in initiating dating relationships and are expected to propose if marriage is to follow. In low gender differentiation cultures, roles beyond procreation are shared by men and women. If men have traditionally behaved in certain ways, women feel comfortable behaving the same way if they desire to do so.

Sweden is a low gender differentiation culture. If Steve is familiar with males and females carrying out different roles in the United States, he is likely so see fewer distinctions in Sweden. After the wife has given birth, for example, men often stay home to raise the children, especially if women have jobs with greater earning capacity. One key to understanding the cultural difference is that there is no disapproval or "raised eyebrows" when people hear about male and female roles. At parties, people are comfortable talking with househusbands and do not cut conversations short to find someone more interesting and important. Marketing campaigns for household products target consumers by featuring attractive men in aprons who are pictured cleaning up the house. The ads are not meant to be humorous. If men are the consumers who use and buy household products, they become the targets of serious advertising campaigns.

The distinction between high and low gender differentiation reminds us that many differences between women are based on cultural expectations, early childhood experiences that men and women are likely to have (Hyde, 2007), and definitions of the self that have been reinforced after years of socialization. Cultures provide explanations for events, and sometimes the explanations reflect views about gender. Many times, these views are not the same in all parts of the world. Views about gender differences in mathematical abilities is a good example (Chatard, Guimond, & Selimbegovic, 2007).

Stereotypes about Women and Mathematics Can Be Dead Wrong

Long a believer in lifelong learning and staff development, Paul Strong offered his staff more advanced training programs than other companies he knew about. Paul was the president of a software development firm in Silicon Valley that had a reputation for being on the cutting edge. He asked members of his extensive network for the names of good trainers who could introduce a variety of technical topics. The name "Ramon Perez" came up frequently, and so Paul asked Ramon to give a workshop on Boolean algebra and discrete mathematics to his programmers.

The workshop went well and Peter met with Ramon to determine how training opportunities could be improved. Ramon commented that several women from Asia were among the best trainees. He mentioned the names of six women who had recently moved to California from Japan, Korea, China, and Thailand. Peter replied that he had been very happy with the job performance of these six people and that others in Silicon Valley had commented that Asian women were among the top programmers.

There is a cultural difference involved when discussions arise about women and mathematics. Boys and girls everywhere complain about how hard math is, and the cultural difference occurs after the complaints are heard. In the United States, teachers historically told girls that their reaction is common and so perhaps they should not take the advanced algebra course next semester. Boys were told of the many careers that demand good math knowledge and so were encouraged to take the advanced course. As a result, more boys than girls found themselves in advanced mathematics courses.

In Asia, teachers don't make a distinction in their reactions to boys and girls. All students are told to stop complaining and to work harder. The teachers may say, "You have not been doing well with 100 homework problems a night, and so I will assign 200 problems." Sometimes, with the encouragement of their involved parents, students request more homework. Performance in mathematics is viewed as due to effort rather than to abilities that some people have but that others don't. If teachers view math as effort-based rather than ability-based, they have advice to give to students: Work harder!!

With their background in advanced mathematics, people from Asia are able to benefit from advanced training programs such as those offered in Peter's company.

Teachers in the United States now recognize this historical difference in their reactions to complaints about mathematics. They are now careful to offer equal encouragement to both boys and girls concerning advanced coursework.

DATING RELATIONSHIPS THAT START AT WORK

When the combination of words "male, female, and workplace" are mentioned, most people immediately think of relationships that might lead to dating relationships and romances. If these relationships do not go well, there may be implications for the workplace if the people involved in past romances prefer not to work together. Additional complexity is added when intercultural interactions are added to the mix. Problems arise when there are cultural differences surrounding concepts such as "a social life" and "a first date." If people bring different meanings to these concepts, there can be unforeseen consequences (Jackson, Chen, Guo, & Gao, 2006).

The Reactions of People after the First Date

Jack Simmons, originally from Chicago, had accepted a position with the branch of a multinational manufacturing firm in Shanghai, China. He had studied Chinese in college and, while not fluent, was able to keep up his end of conversations in a good-natured imperfect manner. Given his outgoing personality, he found himself invited out to dinner in groups of eight or ten colleagues from work. After a few months, he found himself talking with a member of these dinner groups, Haiyan Chan, an accountant at the firm. Haiyan was interested in improving her English and enjoyed chatting with Jack.

One afternoon, Jack saw that Haiyan was alone at her desk. He walked over to her and asked her out to dinner and a performance of the Shanghai circus, which he had seen on television back in Chicago. Haiyan accepted the invitation and they had a good time during their evening out. Back at work the next week, people behaved differently toward Jack. Other women with whom he used to exchange pleasantries, for example, treated Jack in a slightly more formal manner.

The possible misunderstanding here is that Haiyan and others in the workplace consider that Jack is now involved in a serious relationship. Jack feels that he simply had a "first date" to get to know Haiyan better. The cultural difference is that in China, and in many other countries in Asia, any move toward a one-on-one evening out is considered an important step toward a romance. In everyday terms, a first date is a "big deal!" Other people interpret a first date, where two people go out unaccompanied by others, as the sign of a blossoming romance.

Can Americans working in Asia have a social life? The answer is "yes," but they must be prepared to go out in large groups. In the incident, Jack showed cultural awareness by beginning his social life in groups of eight or ten, but he was unaware of how the move to a one-on-one date would be interpreted. If he knew this piece of cultural information, there would be additional considerations to challenge his cultural sensitivity. He would have to ask himself if he was being fair to Haiyan, and to her family and friends, if he suggests the move to a dating relationship.

The fact that people's social lives take place in large groups has interesting implications that can be seen in large cities all over the world where people can choose from a variety of ethnic restaurants. In what types of restaurants are there large round tables that seat eight or ten? In what types of restaurants are there smaller tables for tete-a-tete conversations among two people? "Chinese" comes to mind for the first question, and "French and Italian" for the second. One of my colleagues was turned away from a restaurant in Beijing when he and his wife asked for a table. "Too much trouble for just two," he was told. If there are eight or ten people at a table, they have to speak loudly to be heard by everyone else. This means that "softness and quietness" is not expected, and so the clink-clank-clunk of carts and plates in Chinese restaurants, in sharp contrast to the relative quiet of other restaurants, becomes more understandable.

When people communicate, they have goals. People also have goals when they decide not to communicate. In some cultures, if men and women begin to communicate on a regular basis, others see this as a step toward a romantic relationship. If people do not want to have others think in this way, women and men may keep their conversations short.

The Desire for Minimal Male–Female Interactions

"I wonder if she would like to practice her English," Garth Davis thought to himself as he looked across the office floor and saw Hisako Yoshimura. Garth, from Baltimore, Maryland, had been hired by the Ichiban Computer Software Company in Nagoya, Japan. Hisako worked there as a receptionist. Recently, Garth learned that Hisako had traveled extensively and had earned a college degree from Cambridge University in England. Garth walked over to Hisako's desk, tried to engage her in conversation, but was completely unsuccessful. He wondered if he had made some kind of cultural blunder in recent weeks that would lead to difficulties interacting with Japanese colleagues.

Even though Hisako may want to interact with Garth, she may be reticent given her knowledge of Japanese culture. Generally, there is less opposite sex social interaction during teenage years in Japan compared to the United States. There are fewer school dances and much less one-on-one dating. Many Japanese young adults, then, do not interact smoothly in casual conversations with members of the opposite sex. When a specific male does interact with a specific female and the communication seems to be comfortable and pleasant, observers often conclude that the two are "a romantic item." Hisasko may not return Garth's efforts at conversation since she does not want coworkers to come to this conclusion about their status.

Further, Hisako realizes that if she interacts frequently with Garth she may receive hints from her boss that it is time she got married. Japanese young adults often meet their future spouses in their workplace but spend little time interacting during the workday. Instead, they meet at restaurants that attract an interesting niche market comprised of dating couples who want to hide their romantic relationships from coworkers. These restaurants are often twenty miles away from their office and are chosen to limit the possibilities of being seen by coworkers and friends. If the restaurants are dark and crowded, so much the better.

I have discussed this incident with a number of Japanese nationals. They point to other issues that women like Hisako face. If she received a degree from Cambridge, Hisako's English has to be very good. But if she is heard speaking English fluently with Garth, Japanese men in the organization may feel threatened. All Japanese students study English, but they learn more English grammar (e.g., prepositions and verb tenses) than everyday conversational skills. Hisako may want to hide her English language skills to increase her chances of interactions with Japanese men.

There are various aspects of people's goals and past experiences that will have an effect on the points raised in this incident. Hisako works in Nagoya, a city where there are relatively few Americans like Garth who are in a position to chat with her on a regular basis. If Hisako worked in Tokyo, or in nearby Yokohama where many American military personnel live, she may be very accustomed talking with Americans. Further, since there are so many Americans, there may not be any special meaning attributed to her when she speaks with them.

QUALITY OF LIFE: FAMILY AND INTERPERSONAL RELATIONSHIPS

Japan is a culture with a high degree of gender differentiation. There are role expectations for both men and women, and there is not a great deal of overlap. This is a point to keep in mind when thinking about the preceding incident involving Misako and Garth. There are socially imposed limits as to what she can do and still be looked upon favorably by others. If she was in a low gender differentiated culture, she could talk with Garth and few people would give it a second thought.

Another aspect of low gender differentiation is that women have had an impact on cultural values. If the roles of men and women overlap, then members of both sexes can engage in such behaviors as speaking out, sharing their opinions, seeking jobs in companies with policies consistent with their values, and so forth. In low gender differentiated cultures, then, women have been able to share their ideas and to insist that their values be respected. One of these values is that the quality of life is as important as the quantity of material resources that people can acquire. Quality of life issues include time for family, a balance between work and family commitments, good interpersonal relationships with others, and a cooperative atmosphere in the workplace. Over many generations, both men and women learn to value quality of life issues in low gender differentiated cultures. This distinction between quantity and quality of life issues is central to the analysis of this incident.

American Workaholics Can Be Baffled by Other Cultures

"Three countries in five days. I think I can do it!" Greg Randall said to himself as he waited at the airport in Frankfort, Germany. Greg represented a sporting goods manufacturer and had recently negotiated contracts at two department stores in Paris, and after Frankfort was scheduled for meetings in Amsterdam, Holland. Greg was from Chicago and was one of the most successful salespeople in his company.

Greg was scheduled to meet with Jan De Jong about an hour after his scheduled arrival in Amsterdam. Due to a plane delay, he did not arrive until 5:00 P.M. on a Friday afternoon. He hoped that Jan would still be at his office phone, but this was not the case.

He called Jan at home to schedule a meeting for Saturday, pointing out that it should take only about one-half hour to finalize the deal. Jan said that he could not meet since he promised to take his two preteenage children to the zoo on Saturday. Greg was upset that he would have to stay in Amsterdam until Monday.

Greg has encountered differences in the cultural emphasis on the quantity versus the quality of life. In some cultures, career success is measured by the quantity of outcomes such as salary, number of contracts signed, and the number of promotions received by a certain age. In other cultures, judgments of success include additional outcomes such as time spent with family, the nurturance of hobbies, and sensitivity to the needs of other people. Holland is a country where people emphasize these types of quality issues. Jan has promised a weekend outing with his children. This is a commitment that Greg should respect.

What might Greg do? He could go to the zoo with Jan and his family. He might find a half-hour time slot, while the children are watching the chimpanzees, during which he can close the deal. Even if this is impossible, Greg would show his sensitivity to Jan's culture and this will pay benefits in future business dealings.

Countries that emphasize the quality of life often have social policies that encourage strong families. For example, these countries have "paternity leave" policies where fathers can take paid time from work after the birth of a child. Benefits such as maternity leave, paid day care for children, and extensive social services for the needy are other features of countries such as The Netherlands. These benefits are expensive, however, and tax rates are often much higher than people in "quantity oriented" countries are willing to pay.

If time with family and friends is important, as it is in low gender differentiation countries such as The Netherlands, then behavioral norms should develop that foster good interpersonal relationships. One such norm is that people should develop a soft, modest public demeanor so that they do not step on the toes of others. Further, if people are modest when thinking about their accomplishments, then they are less likely to be the targets of jealous reactions from others.

Modest Self-Presentations Have Advantages in Some Cultures

As part of an program encouraging the short term exchange of executives within a multinational organization headquartered in New York, Hans De Kerk and Roy Nolan found themselves working together on the company newsletter. Hans was from The Hague, Netherlands and was a respected executive with expertise in economic forecasting. Roy, originally from Atlanta, was in the human resources division and also was in charge of editing the company newsletter. He asked Hans to write an article comparing different forecasting models.

Hans turned in an article, Roy edited it, and then gave it back to Hans. Unhappy with some of the changes, Hans came to Roy's office. Roy asked, "What changes didn't you like?" Hans gave an example. He originally wrote, "As many economists have suggested, I find myself agreeing with the importance of examining bounded rationality." Roy had changed this to, "I feel that the analysis of bounded rationality is important." Hans pointed out that he was uncomfortable with the emphasis on "I" as the first word in the revised sentences. Roy replied that the revised sentence was more direct and to the point.

Hans and Roy are bringing a cultural difference to this interaction. The Netherlands is a country where the quality of life is emphasized. Time spent with friends and family is very important. There is a value placed on a comfortable living standard for everyone rather than on a lavish lifestyle for a small number of people. This value is served if people are modest in their self-presentations and do not attempt to stand out and to call special attention to themselves. The emphasis is on the thought, "All Dutch should be equal" rather than, "There are special people who merit massive amounts of attention and money." In school, Dutch children are taught to avoid sentences starting with "I feel" or "I think" because they would call too much attention to themselves.

A modest self-presentation has the additional advantage of protecting people from one of the disadvantages associated with a "quality of life" culture. If everyone should have a similar living standard, there will be jealousy displayed toward those people who acquire wealth and status through talent and hard work. For example, Dutch authors of well-received books may earn considerable amounts of money through royalties. They can avoid being the targets of jealousy if they maintain the same lifestyle and modest self-presentation as they did before their successful publishing ventures.

9

Status and Power

STATUS AND POWER: RELATIVE AMOUNTS OF DIFFERENCE BETWEEN SOCIETAL LEVELS

All cultures have hierarchies in which some people have more status and power than others (Osland & Bird, 2000). Because of the facts surrounding their birth or because of their achievements, some people are marked as individuals to whom others should defer. These elite people have more privileges than others, and they can expect their directives to be followed by those beneath them in their culture's social hierarchy.

The presence of status and power differences is universal. Like many aspects of culture, distinctions exist in the degree to which power and status differ among societal levels. Imagine an eight-foot stepladder. The bottom rung represents people who do not have titles that give them special status. Different cultures have different terms for these individuals. Serfs, peons, peasants, commoners, and working stiffs are just a few. Higher rungs of the ladder represent higher status groups. All cultures have such groups, variously called bosses, managers, governors, senators, presidents, and so forth. The distinction among cultures is the relative amount of distance between people. In some cultures, the difference corresponds to one or two rungs. In other cultures, where status and power are taken more seriously, the difference corresponds to four or five rungs.

Cultures corresponding to one or two rungs of the ladder are called low power distant. For example, people in the United States, compared to other parts of the world, have small distances between power levels. Let's explore some workplace examples. There are certainly bosses and managers, and they have the right to set workplace policies, evaluate workers, and promote those who are making the most contributions to a company. But the distinction between status levels is relatively small. Bosses and workers might address each other using first names. They may socialize outside the workplace on the tennis court or on the golf course. They may do volunteer work together for the same community organizations. Workers do not feel as if they are less worthwhile individuals. They do not view bosses as a special class of individuals to whom deference is automatically granted (Hofstede, 2001). In fact, workers often think that the bosses better do a good job or else they will be replaced in a couple of years. And the replacements may be today's workers who one day will supervise today's bosses!

Cultures corresponding to four or five ladder rungs are called high power distant.

As a generalization, high power distance is found in Asian countries. In the workplace, bosses are given a great deal of deference. Workers rarely disagree with their bosses in public because such behavior is considered disrespectful. Often, workers feel that bosses are better people and deserve the deference they receive because of their personal qualities, not just their job titles. Workers do not view themselves as one day supervising the people who happen to be their bosses today.

There are various behaviors that mark low and high distant cultures. In the United States, for example, comedians make handsome livings telling jokes about powerful people such as the president and prominent institutions such as Congress.

In high power distant cultures, workers engage in gestures such as standing when bosses enter a room or accompanying them to the train station prior to a business trip. Students retain a lifelong deference to their professors, referring to themselves as the junior person even if they have more career success than their old professors.

When people accept international assignments, adjustments to the differing importance of status and power can be challenging (Littrell, 2007). People moving from low to high power distant cultures must be much more respectful of their bosses and must defer to their wishes. People moving from high to low power distant cultures must learn to treat bosses as near equals or else they will develop reputations for being toadies and sycophants.

Korea is a high power distant culture. The American in this incident learned that he cannot behave in the same way toward his Korean boss as he behaved toward his Korean friends during his college years.

Respect for Power Holders Is Highly Valued in Some Cultures

"I think my last conversation with our boss did not go very well," Martin Summers told colleagues as they ate lunch together in the company cafeteria. Martin, thirty years old, had accepted a position as a computer specialist at an accounting firm in Taejon, Korea. It was a dream job for Martin. He had studied Korean for four years in college. Given his outgoing personality and obvious interest in Asia, he was welcomed by international students from Korea and spent much of his free time associating with them. He was able to practice conversational Korean with these students, and this helped him excel in his classroom studies.

His boss in Korea was Jung-Ho Cho. A graduate of Seoul National University, Jung-Ho was thirty-five years old, looked young for his age, and seemed to have a sense of humor when he discussed company issues with members of his staff. One day, Martin made an appointment with Jung-Ho to recommend the purchase of some expensive software. Martin tried to remember how he interacted with his Korean friends at college when he made a recommendation to them. He tried to use memories of previous successful approaches during this conversation with Jung-Ho.

When Martin remembers his college years, he will be remembering informal interactions with Koreans. These interactions among age peers are not what Martin should have in mind when he interacts with his boss. The Korean language has various honorifics that people are expected to use when they interact with high status people. Honorifics include choice of vocabulary terms, a different set of verb endings, and use of a deferential and respectful tone of voice. In contrast, English has relatively few honorifics, and their use can often seem stilted and inappropriate. Many Americans are quite successful using very similar language when talking with bosses, colleagues, and subordinates. Koreans, on the other hand, are very sensitive to the absence of honorifics when they are expected. Bosses, for instance, feel insulted when subordinates do not use language that acknowledges status differences. In addition, Jung-Ho Cho attended Seoul National University, one of Korea's most prestigious schools. He is likely to be accustomed to receiving deference just because he attended this school.

Language use that acknowledges status distinctions is part of cultural differences in power distance. In some cultures such as the United States, the psychological distance between bosses and subordinates is small. The subordinates do not feel that their bosses are better people, often address bosses using first names, and look forward to the day when they will be bosses. In other cultures such as Korea, the psychological distance is much greater. Bosses are highly respected, receive deference from their subordinates, and are often viewed as role models for proper behavior according to Korean social norms. Respect for this power distance is communicated when subordinates use honorifics during interactions with their bosses.

Sensitivity to status differences is necessary in all kinds of interactions between bosses and subordinates, and also between people of roughly equal status. In the following incident, the visiting American has a great deal of status because of his career accomplishments, and he must interact with Japanese executives. So who has the most status and engages in high status activities like speaking first or sitting at the most prominent place at the dinner table? Here, my advice is to go with the heuristic that there is a "home court advantage" and that high status visitors should defer to host executives.

Negotiating Status Hierarchies in Different Countries

Because he had recently been awarded a patent in wireless user interface technology, Bob Mayer had received extensive publicity in his hometown, Seattle, Washington. Known locally as "the twenty-four-year-old boy wonder," Bob felt that there were international markets for his technology. He scheduled a trip to Osaka, Japan, to have meetings at Sumitomo Electronics. He was pleased to learn that his reputation preceded him given extensive coverage of his patent in the *Asian Wall Street Journal* and the *Japan Times*. The chairman of the board asked Tadashi Ueda, a vice president at Sumitomo, to welcome Bob and to arrange a meeting with ten other influential executives. Tadashi was fifty years old and was well known at Sumitomo for his twenty-five years of excellent work.

Tadashi met Bob in his office and they walked together to a meeting room where the other executives were waiting. When they came to the door, they both stopped, wondering who should enter first. Both knew the general guideline that the higher status person should enter first, but it was unclear who this was. Bob was very young but had status because of his well-publicized patent. Tadashi had status as an older man who was a company vice president. Bob and Tadashi stood at the door to the meeting room and looked to each other for guidance concerning what to do next.

Bob and Tadashi are engaging in "status abacus." They are trying to figure out who has the higher status so that the culturally appropriate behavior, entering the room first, can take place. The process is complex in this example since the two people bring different kinds of status to their encounters. Bob has his youthful major achievements, and Tadashi has his age and company title. The former carries weight in the United States, and the latter is important in Japan.

Bob should consider ways of showing knowledge of Japan's "home court advantage." For instance, he might say, "Please go first. I'm just a guest here and you're the vice president." Even if he does not behave in ways that are totally appropriate in Japan, his efforts to be culturally sensitive will be recognized and appreciated. If people can communicate goodwill and an appreciation of cultural differences, minor errors during social and work encounters will often be forgiven.

THE DUTIES ACCOMPANYING HIGH STATUS POSITIONS

To maintain their high status and to obtain continual respect, power-holders must engage in behaviors that meet the expectations of subordinates. They must appear very knowledgeable, must carry themselves in a way that generates confidence among observers, and they must accept the trappings of power such as large offices with expensive furnishings. Another expectation, especially in Asia, is that bosses behave in a paternal manner toward their subordinates. They must be seen as caring, and must be willing to offer advice concerning subordinates' personal lives. Keep in mind that bosses are given a great deal of deference, and some of this deference is because of the supposed wisdom bosses possess toward many aspects of life.

Leadership Styles in Asia are Often Highly Personalized

"The size of this company and the one I used to work for in Korea is about the same," Sook Ki Kim told Paul Kincaid. Sook Ki previously worked for an investment firm in Pusan, Korea, and recently accepted a position in international finance at a firm in Omaha, Nebraska. Paul was the president of the firm in Omaha where 150 people were on the payroll.

After three months on the job, Sook Ki asked for an appointment with Paul. There were no problems with her work, she said, but she was beginning to have difficulties in her personal life. Her children were not doing well in school, probably because they were still learning English. Her husband had to accept a job in Omaha that was not at the level of his professional qualifications in Korea. Given these stresses, family members were not happy with their lives in America. Sook Ki asked Paul for his advice concerning what to do. Paul felt unprepared and unqualified to give such advice.

Sook Ki and Paul have different views of what managers and leaders are expected to do. In the United States, leaders give advice on professional issues, and Paul would be comfortable giving Sook Ki guidance on how to keep up-to-date with developments in American financial markets. However, he may be very uncomfortable giving personal advice. If there was a Human Resources Department in his organization, he would probably refer Sook Ki to a specialist who has had training and experience on how to help with employees' personal problems.

In Korea and other Asian countries, leaders are often expected to be sources of excellent advice on personal issues. Leadership is sometimes referred to as "own family and personal." Leaders are expected to treat employees as members of their family and to treat them in highly personalized ways. This emphasis on the personal life means that leaders know about employees' families. They know the ages of employees' children, what schools they are going to, what their spouses do, and what problems family members are having with various aspects of their lives. Leaders are expected to have good advice on personal matters and employees take this advice very seriously.

This own family/personal style is more common in small firms than in very large organizations. If a company has more than 500 employees, the company president cannot be expected to have personal information about everyone. In large organizations, however, the role of personal advice giver may be taken on by a department head in charge of fifty or sixty people. If managers are expected to offer advice about life outside the workplace, they will lose the respect of coworkers if they are unwilling to assume this responsibility.

THE DISTRIBUTION OF RESOURCES

When managers and their bosses are successful, there may be profits that can be distributed among an organization's personnel. There are cultural differences in how profits are commonly divided and how people view the distribution as fair or unfair (Schwartz, 2007). In high power distant countries, it is wise to take care of powerful people and to make sure that they reap the benefits of company success. The benefits do not always have to be monetary. Other forms of recognition, such as testimonial dinners and use of powerful people's names as project titles (e.g., the Jung-Ho Cho Executive Building) may serve the purpose of deferring to high status people. When profits are to be distributed among a group of workers at roughly the same status level, the distribution can be based on either equality or equity, as in this incident.

Equality and Equity When Recognizing Employee Contributions

"The procedure I used to recognize high performing employees worked when I introduced it in Boston," Dan Romney told colleagues at an executive retreat. "The same system bombed here in Osaka." Dan had been an executive at a multinational bank in Osaka, Japan, for a year. When working in Boston, he distributed company profits by identifying the best employees and rewarding them according to their contributions. If people worked hard and were clearly contributing to organizational goals, they received more end-of-year benefits than average-performing employees. Dan's approach proved popular and was adopted by other executives in various American branches of the bank.

When Dan tried to introduce a similar system in Osaka, it proved to be very unpopular. Employees who received year-end bonuses did not seem appreciative, and Dan felt that morale in his division had decreased. He could not figure out why his incentive system worked in one country but not the other.

Dan has encountered a cultural difference in the relative emphasis placed on equity and equality in the distribution of employee benefits. If executives set up systems based on equity, they identify high-performing people and reward them more than average-performing employees. With equity, attempts are made to reward people based on their individual contributions. Employees who contribute more, for example by bringing in more business to the bank, are rewarded more.

If executives set up systems based on equality, they make attempts to give similar amounts of rewards to all employees. The emphasis in an equality-based system is to recognize the work of all employees, not a smaller number of high performers. Equality based systems are common in collectivist cultures, such as Japan, where there is great value placed on being a member of a group. If one or two people receive more rewards than others, this may interfere with group harmony. High performers themselves become uncomfortable if they are centered out for special attention. Employees justify equality with statements such as, "Yes, there were some outstanding performers this year. But next year, other employees may be outstanding. It is best to look at the contributions of the group over the long run."

There may be some changes in the future. Japanese employees may become more attentive to their own careers and may downplay company loyalty. The promise of lifetime employment in Japan has been weakened by the Asian economic crisis. Companies have instituted layoffs. College graduates do not have the range of choices among jobs that they did twenty years ago. Japanese businesspeople might become more attentive to keeping up good resumes, and a listing as "employee of the year" is an attractive entry.

In addition to serving the traditional goals of collectivism, maintaining harmony, and reducing the possibility of jealousy, an equal distribution of rewards serves the goals of bosses in a high power distant culture such as Japan. With equal distribution among workers at the same level, bosses retain their high status over a relatively undifferentiated group of subordinates. In addition, an equal distribution of rewards insures that subordinates will not have practice using negotiation and other political skills. If people are to have an equitable distribution, they have to negotiate how this will be done. This process will favor people with good communication skills and will favor people with good political alliances in the organization. The subordinates who are best at these negotiations may eventually threaten the status of power holders. With an equal distribution of rewards, people have far less need to develop or to practice their political skills.

A DOWNSIDE OF POWER: INTOXICATION AND ABUSE

Another universal aspect of power is that there is always the danger that people will become intoxicated with it and that they will abuse their subordinates. In high power distant cultures, subordinates often have to tolerate abusive power holders. In low power distant cultures, subordinates have a slightly easier time challenging high status people. They can complain to a company human resources department or to their union, contact influential members of a company's board of directors, or complain to people in the organization who are higher in status than the abusive boss.

Sometimes, it is difficult for executives at the highest level of a company to identify abusive midlevel managers because their behavior is different depending upon the status of the people with whom they are dealing.

Some People are Careful to Fit Themselves into Authority Structures

"I never thought I would have a meeting like this," Judy Higgins said to the president of the office supplies company where she worked. The president, Carol Ness, recognized Judy's discomfort and encouraged her to talk freely. Judy worked in sales and traveled extensively to represent the company. She told Carol that she was having a very difficult time with her direct supervisor, Carl Hagen. "He shouts at people to the point of being abusive, never says anything good about their work, takes credit for the work of others, and has no sense of a collegial, cooperative sales force." Carol listened carefully but said, "I'm surprised at this report. Carl has always been extremely cooperative and respectful in meetings with me."

Carl Hagen may have an authoritarian personality. Some people are very aware of status, power, and authority relations in the workplace. They view their subordinates as less able than themselves. "Given this lesser ability, my subordinates should pay attention to what I want done and behave according to my directives." They often don't feel the need to show their appreciation. Rather, they feel that workers should be grateful that they are allowed to remain in the company and that they receive their paychecks.

The sometimes less visible aspect of authoritarians is that they are very deferent and polite in the presence of their superiors. This follows from the general point that they want acceptance from powerful, high-status people. They feel it is wise to court the favor of these more powerful people, and they do this with politeness and deference. In this incident, Carol is surprised to hear about Carl's behavior because it is at odds with her interactions with him. Carol has not seen Carl's behaviors that occur outside of her presence: abusive behavior toward subordinates. The combination of "suck up" to superiors and "dump down" on subordinates is the hallmark of the authoritarian personality.

Authoritarians can be found in all countries. They may survive as middle managers longer in high power distant countries where workers are not encouraged to complain about how they are treated. In such countries, workers are discouraged from jumping levels in the company hierarchy and going directly to the company president, as Judy did with Carol. In low power distant countries, depending on company policies, authoritarian managers can sometimes be disciplined for creating a hostile, stress-filled, and unproductive work environment. In the long run, authoritarian managers often are losers. They make so many enemies that they have no support group and no letter of recommendation writers when they are being considered for promotions or for executive positions at other companies.

OBTAINING STATUS AND POWER: RESOURCES AND NETWORKS

If people aspire to positions of power and status, they must nurture or develop resources that they can exchange with other power holders. Some resources are available at birth and so should be nurtured and not squandered. These include a prestigious family name, family money, and relatives with good contacts in their communities. Other resources are not necessarily available at birth but, at least for people who are not the victims of societal discrimination, can be obtained through personal effort. These include education, skills that are needed in society, and the willingness to contribute to the efforts of others in anticipation of returned favors in the future.

Some ethnic groups who are very aware of discrimination in the past develop the norm that it is important to get a good education. This is seen as the road to advancement, and it is also a resource that others cannot take away.

Emphasis on Intellectual Achievement Starts during Childhood

"You might talk to Kevin about joining the softball team that will challenge other company-sponsored teams at the city-wide picnic," Grace Ridley told Sol Greenberg. "But remember that Kevin takes his softball very seriously." Sol replied, "My guess is that Kevin could do a lot better than me for his team. I never developed baseball/softball skills as a kid. There was a good youth sports program in my community, but my parents emphasized homework, extra reading beyond assigned work, and Hebrew classes at the Temple. Will there be a Jeopardy-type game at the picnic with a lot of questions about history?"

Sol's memories about his childhood are common among Jewish people. Education is highly valued, and so children's attention to homework takes precedence over community activities such as youth sports. The emphasis on education is a prominent part of Jewish culture. Given a long history of anti-Semitism and the frequency of pogroms, Jewish people are very sensitive about how they are viewed by others. Jewish parents often tell their children about their history and at the same time emphasize the future. "They can take away our money, they can take away our homes, but they cannot take away our education. This is why it is so important to be as well-educated as you can be." With this attention to doing well in school, Jewish people receive the education necessary to take their place among physicians, lawyers, journalists, university professors, and other professionals. This emphasis leads to ethnic jokes that Jewish people share among themselves. A woman had two sons, the president of the United States and a medical doctor. The medical doctor had set up a practice in the Washington, DC, area. She told a friend that she would be visiting Washington. The friend asked, "It's so exciting that you will be visiting your son in the White House!" The mother replied, "No, I'm visiting my son the doctor."

One of my Jewish colleagues tells this story. He did well in high school and began to talk about taking a few years off to travel abroad and to get some work experience. One of his uncles asked him, "Do you really want to be the first person in your family who drops out of school and doesn't immediately go from high school to college? Do you want to be known as the family member who killed his father?" My colleague went to college and later received his doctoral degree.

I first became aware of this cultural emphasis when I was fourteen years old. There was a religious retreat to which all Boy Scout troops in Western Massachusetts were invited. Troops put together teams that would answer questions about the Bible. The team I was on finished second to a troop sponsored by a synagogue. While there were many questions about the Old Testament, at least half of the questions asked were about events and people in the New Testament. I remember saying to myself, "We were beat fair and square, and there must be something in the winning troop's education that allowed them to do so well."

Another way to enter high status positions is to have a good network of influential people (Oh, Chung, & Labianca, 2004). Networking may be more common in individualistic cultures where people do not have strong ties to a permanent collective and so have time and energy to develop loose but important ties with power holders (Triandis, 1995). Networking is often difficult for collectivists working in individualistic cultures since they do not have extensive experience meeting strangers, putting them at their ease, and exchanging information that might lead to future interactions that will benefit all parties involved (Toyokawa, 2006).

People in the Same Network Trade Favors for Goal Accomplishment

"The market for hand-made collectibles is increasing here in the Pacific Northwest," John Shore told Taufik Pekerti as they looked at samples of fabric art from various Asian countries. John was a division manager of an import company in Tacoma, Washington, and Taufik was a representative for a handicraft guild in Jakarta, Indonesia. When John had visited Jakarta six months ago, Taufik had been very helpful introducing him to various business associates. Now, John could return the favor since Taufik had traveled to Tacoma with the hopes of finding new markets for the guild's products.

John took Taufik to dinner and they discussed various business opportunities. John mentioned that there was a reception in two days for a visiting university professor who would be presenting information on Internet marketing to an invited audience. "Maybe you'd like to come," John added. "There will also be a reception. The networking opportunities should be very good." Taufik did not know what John meant since he had never heard the term "networking" used in this context.

If a person has a good network, it means that he or she knows many other people who can be of assistance on various aspects related to work. A good network has people from different fields: journalism, politics, law, accounting, marketing, psychology, and so forth. People in networks trade favors. One person might offer help on a marketing plan in return for later help finding a good motivational speaker for a convention of business professionals. People in active networks also refer customers to each other, keep each other apprised of political developments that can impact business, and pass on information about attractive investment possibilities.

Network members are not necessarily good friends who are part of each other's emotional lives. Members do not necessarily have relationships that go back many years. Rather, network membership can be developed quickly as long as people have a reason to interact and to keep in touch. At the reception, Taufik may meet people who can help him achieve his goals of opening up new markets. To be a good network member, he has to keep in mind that he must return favors. For example, he might share the names of influential government officials in Asia who will be of assistance if Americans want to investigate various overseas business opportunities.

Taufik may be less familiar with networking than John. As an Indonesian, Taufik was socialized into a collectivist culture. Collectivists have relations with people that have developed over many years: relatives, business associates of their fathers, college classmates, and so forth. If Taufik needs business contacts or information, he is likely to approach his long-term collective. John, on the other hand, will be comfortable approaching a network member whom he met only a few days ago.

STATUS MARKERS

As part of networking and the pursuit of influence in their communities, people often are attentive to the trappings of status. These trappings are culturally influenced, that is, different cultures have different signs and signals that people have high status. If people have these markers, others can say to themselves, "This person is worth my time."

Different Status Symbols Communicate "I've Arrived!"

"Why do you continue to raise cattle when you are losing so much money?" Gloria Sanchez had recently met Matt Dunham, owner of the very successful "Big D" restaurant in Dallas, Texas. Gloria had recently moved to Dallas after graduating from Dartmouth College in New Hampshire. Matt had told Gloria that he owned a herd of cattle on a ranch about fifty miles outside Dallas, but he added that it was a big money loser. His explanation that both his father and grandfather had owned cattle seemed incomplete to Gloria.

There are status symbols in different parts of the United States that tell others, "I have been successful." This is one advantage to owning a ranch in Texas. This activity tells others, "I have made enough money to engage in raising cattle, a highly valued tradition with a rich history in Texas." People make money in businesses such as oil, construction, electronics, or retailing. In Texas, however, these businesses carry less status than ranching. Texans sometimes say, "You have to be rich to even consider raising cattle." The message of this comment is similar to the joke shared by musicians.

Question: How do end up with a million dollars in the music business?
Answer: Start with two million dollars.

There are status symbols in other parts of the country. Expensive Country Club memberships exist in most medium sized and big cities. In Northern New England, ownership of ski equipment and clothing that follow fashion trends rather than the requirements of the sport communicate high status. In cities along ocean coastlines, owning a yacht signals success, even if people work so hard that they go sailing only two or three times a year.

In big cities in East Asia, owning an expensive car such as a Mercedes or a Porsche marks high status. In these same cultures, influential women dress in the latest New York or Paris fashions and they wear expensive jewelry. In many Pacific Island cultures, people with high status are able to marshal resources such as food, entertainment, and gifts so that they can throw big parties.

Returning to the Texas example, there are benefits to raising cattle that can have important financial implications. If people own cattle, they can network with other influential and wealthy people. They can go to the cattle auction and chat with others about land deals, various investment opportunities, politics, and the status of budget-related bills in the legislature. But if they don't bid on cattle, they may not be taken seriously and will not be encouraged to participate in serious discussions. People may dress well for the auction, but they may be dismissed as "all hat and no cattle." Texans use this phrase to refer to individuals who have an attractive outward appearance but who cannot follow up this image with substance and achievement.

10

The Number and Importance of Social Norms

SOCIAL NORMS AND THEIR RELATION TO THE FUTURE

Many aspects of culture have developed to deal with problems that are universally faced by all people (House et al., 2004). Such problems include pursuing resources important to one's family without interfering with the rights of others. Another problem is how to deal with a culture's nonrenewable resources and the selection of leaders who have the right to enforce conservation policies. Since children are necessary for cultures to survive, still another universal issue is that people make decisions about desirable and undesirable unions among men and women.

All cultures have norms, or socially agreed upon standards of behavior that mark well-socialized individuals (Chen, Wasti, & Triandis (2007). Distinctions exist regarding the number of norms and the seriousness of consequences should they be broken. The necessity for norms arises from a universal fact. We cannot predict the future. Nobody in a culture knows exactly what the world will look like in twenty years. So there is uncertainty, and this can cause anxiety because people do not know how exactly to prepare for the future (Duronto, Nishida, & Nakayama, 2005). Should they stay in school and receive more formal education, or should they seek work experience? Should they get married now, or put this important decision off for several more years until they have saved more money? There are arguments on both sides of these and hundreds of other questions. Nobody knows for sure.

To deal with uncertainty about the future, cultures develop in various ways. One approach is to develop as many norms as possible. We may not be able to predict all aspects of the future, but with many norms we can be sure that tomorrow's world will bear some resemblance to what is familiar today. Such norms deal with a wide range of behaviors: how men and women meet and interact with each other, workplace punctuality, dress standards, amount of deference shown to bosses, and so forth. These norms might be strictly enforced. People who are late to work and who publicly disagree with superiors can be disciplined. People who break norms concerning male-female interactions may find themselves shunned by others.

Another approach to dealing with an uncertain future is to have as few norms as possible. People don't know exactly what tomorrow will bring, but with few norms they can be flexible when faced with new challenges. If they can't solve problems using one approach they can try another because multiple norms don't force them into rigidity.

Behavioral scientists use the term uncertainty avoidance (Hofstede, 2001; Merkin, 2006) for this analysis of the future and cultural norms. In high uncertainty avoidant cultures, people want to be sure that what is familiar today will be seen in the future. As a result, they have many norms and they are strictly enforced. Japan is a high uncertainty avoidant culture, with many norms guiding behaviors in the school, workplace, and in interactions with other individuals. The United States is a low uncertainty avoidant culture. There are relatively few norms and there is a great deal of slack given to people who break norms.

Complexity can certainly be added to the analysis of culture, norms, and the future. Norms refer to socially agreed upon behaviors. Norms and laws are different. If people do not follow norms, the sanctions are social disapproval. If people do not obey laws, the sanctions are fines or jail time. All cultures have norms and there comes a time everywhere when norm breakers are considered socially unskilled. The analysis of uncertainty avoidance deals with the relative number of norms and the relative seriousness of how norm breakers are treated. Let's look at an example of what happens when a person from a low uncertainty avoidant culture, the United States, accepts a position in a high uncertainty avoidant culture, Japan.

Some Cultures Place Value on Following the Rules

During his orientation program prior to his departure for Osaka, George White learned that executives in Japanese organizations expect employees to engage in after-hours socializing. Originally from Newark, New Jersey,

George had accepted a position at a large Japanese bank. One day, he was invited by colleagues to play golf on the coming Saturday. George looked forward to the golf game given that he liked the sport and felt that he could become better acquainted with his coworkers.

Weather predictions called for a temperature of 100 degrees and 90 percent humidity. George dressed in clothes he had brought with him from New Jersey: a fashionable set of white shorts and a lightweight designer shirt. Arriving at the golf course, George sensed that his Japanese coworkers were uncomfortable. He had learned just enough about Japanese nonverbal signals to realize that he had become the target of disapproval. Eventually, one of his coworkers mentioned that people don't wear shorts at this golf course: the rules call for males to wear long pants. When George asked if this and other rules were written down, his coworkers seemed puzzled by his question.

From their point of view, everyone should know about dress standards at the golf course. In Japan, rules are taken very seriously. One universal aspect of cultures is that the future cannot be predicted with certainty. Two possible responses to this fact are to have many written and unwritten rules so as to increase predictability. People in "rule oriented" cultures can't predict everything, but they can predict those aspects of behavior that are rule-governed. Such behaviors include dress codes, punctuality, ways of interacting harmoniously with others, and the importance of showing respect for superiors. Another response is to have as few rules as possible so that people can be flexible when faced with the future's uncertainties. If people lose their jobs, for example, they can search for new positions in many ways if their culture has relatively few "proper job search rules." Japan is a culture that values rules, while the United States is a culture that values flexibility and adaptability to changing circumstances.

Japanese workers tell this story to each other. A company president informed a group of newly hired employees that the workday is from 8:00 A.M. to 5:00 P.M. and that the employee entrance would be closed at 8:00 A.M. sharp! One day, the president had a flat tire on his way to work and arrived late. He found the employee entrance locked and he would not ask that it be opened. Rules are rules, and he had to follow them since he did not want to be a poor example to his employees.

Another important point is that cultures can change over time. Japan has been described as high uncertainty avoidant, but there are various challenges to this generalization, especially by young people. Many Japanese women are not accepting the traditional norm that they marry and have children before they are thirty years old. Men and women are graduating from college but many are not accepting the norm that they immediately find work in a corporation. Rather, many live at home, support themselves with parttime work, and pursue interests in music, graphic arts, athletics, and entrepreneurial ventures. The collective efforts of many young people may have a major impact on how the Japanese prepare for the future.

THE INFLUX OF NEW IDEAS IN UNCERTAINTY AVOIDANT CULTURES

High uncertainty avoidant cultures have norms for many behaviors, and norms guide behaviors that can be unexpected from the viewpoint of outsiders. For example, cultures can become stagnant if everyone thinks the same way and nobody thinks about new possibilities and improvements to the status quo. But what happens in high power distant cultures? Suggestions for improvements, and protests about current policies, can be seen as disrespectful challenges to power holders. One way around this dilemma is to identify a group of people who, according to social norms, is expected to engage in public protests. In some countries, this task is given to young people during their college years.

Culture and Social Norms: Who Protests against the Status Quo?

Eight years ago, Brad Summers was invited to Seoul, Korea, to speak about leadership development, the topic of his recent best-selling book. One of his interpreters was In-Soo Cha, whose English was excellent. In-Soo, then twenty-two years old, was the son of a diplomat assigned to Washington, DC, and he had attended American public schools as a child. In-Soo was a full-time college student, and he was a leader in the "English Club" at Yonsei University. He found his interpreting skills useful since he was able to meet various Korean businesspeople during his work assignments. Several recommended that he apply to their companies after college graduation and compulsory military service.

Brad and In-Soo found that they had much in common since Brad had worked in the State Department in Washington, DC. Brad also discovered that In-Soo was active in various student protest movements. At the time, students were protesting issues such as the poor qualifications of some political candidates, the future of North Korea, and overly cozy relations with the United States on defense policies. Brad had done his share of protesting earlier in his life (civil rights, Vietnam War), and so enjoyed hearing about In-Soo's experiences as a leader and organizer of student demonstrations.

On a return trip last year, Brad was scheduled to speak at a high technology firm in Pusan. He was given the names of probable attendees, and he noticed In-Soo's name. Brad arrived at the firm early, hoping to speak with In-Soo. The two met, but In-Soo seemed to be a different person. Gone was the protestor of years past. Instead, In-Soo seemed to be the perfect company man: quiet, well dressed, very knowledgeable about high technology developments in Korea, and loyal to company policies.

Brad has encountered an interesting example of cultural roles. A role is a collection of behaviors and ideas that are associated with a title. Titles include husband, boss, politician, parent, and student. In Korea, college students are expected to take on the role of protestors. They are expected to be "the social conscience of the nation" and are expected to call attention to the government's shortcomings. Other aspects of the protestor role are that organizers recruit large numbers of students and encourage them to wear similar uniforms while demonstrating. This shows unity and common effort for the students' recommended action.

All cultures have roles, and they change as people grow older. During his second trip, Brad encountered In-Soo as he approached his thirtieth birthday. His proper role is no longer "protestor against the government." His expected role now is to be a hardworking and loyal worker in his company. Further, he should be married and should have children. The role of protestor will be taken over by the current generation of college students.

GUIDANCE FOR EVERYDAY BEHAVIORS

In high uncertainty avoidant cultures, norms encourage predictability in everyday behaviors. This means that people can plan their days because the behaviors of others with whom they have business dealings, such as shopkeepers, accountants, and medical doctors, are guided by cultural norms. Predictability also means that businesspeople who serve the public can also plan their work day and can be sure that they will have time for other valued aspects of life, such as time with their families and time for hobbies.

Customer Service Reflects Culture in the United States and Germany

When I give workshops dealing with culture and cultural differences, I try to encourage participant involvement as soon as possible. One way is to ask, "All of you have interacted with people from other cultures. Some of you have traveled to other countries. What differences have you observed compared to your own culture?" People from Germany often comment on America's approach to customer service. They point out that stores in the United States are open for many more hours than in Germany. "Back home, stores are open 9:00 A.M. to 5:00 P.M., and people don't expect to do their shopping during evening hours."

There are more consumer products available, and more choices among makes and models of products such as personal computers, cameras, music on compact disks, and home furnishings. Germans also comment that they are often greeted by American salespeople in a much more open, enthusiastic manner. "Hello, how are you today?" is a near-universal greeting in the United States but is heard far less frequently in Germany.

People's everyday behaviors serve their goals. In the United States, people are individualists and they do not want their everyday behaviors restricted by a multitude of social norms. They want to pursue their goals on their own schedules. They also want to be noticeably different from others. These goals are served if stores have many products, have different makes and models of those products, and have generous hours so that people can shop when it is convenient for them. In Germany, there is not as strong an emphasis on individualism and so choices among many makes and models are not as important. Predictability is valued. If stores are open from 9:00 A.M. to 5:00 P.M., then people can arrange their days to allow for shopping. Storeowners and staff can also plan their days. If they close their stores at 5:00 P.M., they will have time for other activities in their lives, especially time with their families.

Questions about "how are you today?" are heard less frequently among Germans. This is captured by another set of norms: the proper use of pronouns. Where English has "you," Germans divide the second person singular into "Sie" and "Du" and make careful distinctions in their use. "Du" is personal and is used for family and friends. "Sie" is more formal and is used for people not well known, such as customers in a store. Germans are not comfortable greeting people for whom "Sie" is appropriate and then asking personal questions.

Americans who move to Germany, or travel there for business or vacation, should know that if Germans begin to ask, "How are you today?" they are likely to be sincere and are interested in the answer.

There are links, then, between uncertainty avoidance and individualism and collectivism. In individualistic cultures, norms develop to serve goals such as the communication that people are unique and that they have interests that not everyone in the culture shares. In collectivistic cultures, people have not been socialized to communicate that they are unique. Rather, their goal is to show others that they can blend their interests into those of others and that they can maintain harmony in groups.

Culture Has an Impact on Everyday Behaviors

Culture gives guidance for everyday behaviors in the presence of norms that children learn as they move through childhood, into their teenage years, and then into adulthood. Culture gives us guidance on acceptable ways of dealing with regularly recurring issues. These include meeting others for the first time, making sales calls, seeking out job interviews, asking others for favors, and competing for promotions within a company. Often, cultures guide people toward quite different behaviors associated with these recurring issues.

For example, an American from Boston may meet a Korean national from Seoul in a multicultural city such as Honolulu. Given her culture's guidance, the American may tell where she went to college, what unique interests she was able to pursue, and what her opinions are concerning current political developments in America and North Korea. Her goal is to communicate that she is a unique individual, and this is a major aspect of her culture. Given his cultural background, the Korean national may talk about points raised by the American and may seek areas of agreement. His goal is not to communicate that he is a unique individual. His goal is to show that he is a cooperative person who values interpersonal harmony.

Difficulties arise when people do not understand this cultural difference and the norms that people learned are appropriate when they meet others for the first time. If they continue their conversation along the same line for fifteen minutes or more, the two people are likely to make contrasting conclusions. The Korean will conclude that the American is self-absorbed and opinionated. The American will conclude that the Korean is a bland and uninteresting individual who does not add anything to conversations. Given their negative attributions, they may not seek out each other's company in the future.

If they understand the cultural difference, however, they will be able to move beyond initial impressions and may be able to appreciate each other's approach to meeting people for the first time. If they decide to interact again, they will likely experience the richness of understanding a wide variety of cultural differences.

This distinction between norms for demonstrating individuality contrasted to norms for showing the capacity for interpersonal harmony is shared by other collectivistic cultures. One of my Japanese colleagues became aware of this difference when he found that during social occasions in the United States, he found people would talk to him for a few minutes but would then seek out someone else at the gathering. He figured out the cultural difference and then practiced before a mirror. He would introduce himself to the figure in the mirror, mention his specific interests and opinions on various current events, and would then ask the other person to tell about himself or herself. After finding topics of mutual interest, my Japanese colleague would focus on those during the conversation. After learning to communicate in this way, my colleague found himself invited to lots of social gatherings.

Clearly, sojourners need to learn a different set of social norms if they are to adjust successfully to other cultures. They also need to know the goals that norms serve.

The critical incidents in this chapter have dealt with various goals: predictability, allowing for the expression of new ideas, communicating uniqueness contrasted with the ability to integrate one's interests with those of others, and developing a social life.

Another goal directing many norms is the ability to show company loyalty, as in this example.

Relations between Reporters and Sources are Affected by Culture

"This article about Japanese unemployment doesn't tell me very much," John Pierce said to himself as he was reading one of Japan's major daily newspapers. John was originally from Boston, now worked in Tokyo in the travel industry, and spoke fluent Japanese. He later complained to a friend, "There is good coverage of statistics, but no treatment of how people are reacting to increasing unemployment. I want to know how college students feel about competing for fewer job openings, if personnel directors of organizations have to turn away good applicants, and what Japanese executives think about government plans for improving the economy."

John's reaction is based on cultural differences in people's willingness to talk to individuals who are outside their immediate circle of friends and acquaintances. For most people, newspaper reporters who call them on the phone are relative strangers. The question becomes, "Will I open up to this reporter and tell her what I think and feel about the subject matter she is investigating?" In the United States, the answer is "yes" often enough that reporters can interview many people and can include direct quotes in their newspaper articles. Since he is from Boston, where several newspapers compete for readership, John is accustomed to this type of media coverage.

In Japan, people are much more reticent to talk with people whom they do not already know. Further, they are socialized not to cause difficulties and not to stand out from their peers. Every Japanese child learns the adage, "The nail that sticks up gets hammered down!" Japanese children learn to value cooperation and to downplay dissention. They learn to set aside their own disagreements within their group so that harmony is maintained. If Japanese businesspeople talk to reporters, they know they may be asked to reveal confidential information about their companies, and they may view this as disloyalty. If Japanese college students talk to reporters about their job searches, they fear being marked as whiners and complainers whom no company will hire.

This difference between Americans and Japanese is sometimes called "the blab factor." One reason the United States has a vigorous free press is that reporters cultivate sources in their communities. The sources are willing to talk for various reasons: outrage at corrupt practices, revenge for past negative experiences in their companies, feelings of status and power that a person has sensitive information that others desire, and a desire to help reporters with whom they now have personal relationships. Without information from such sources, many important issues could not be reported to the general public. An editor once told me, "People often ask why we don't cover certain controversial issues. Is it because we are wimps? The answer is 'no!' We will cover issues if we have accurate information. But that information is often based on the willingness of insider sources to come forward."

UNCERTAINTY AVOIDANCE AND STRESS

An uncertainty about the future causes stress. Hofstede (2001) suggested that to deal with stress, people develop norms so that there will be predictability and consequently some reduction in stress. Put another way, if a culture has a large number of norms, those aspects of stress due to unpredictability will be lessened. Examples of such norms are how to behave toward bosses in the workplace, dress standards for social gatherings sponsored by one's organization, and the number of years a person should work at a company before going up for promotion. If normative standards are well-established, people can reduce the stress of making decisions about these issues by following the norms. But complexities must be added since there is the danger of a vicious cycle. Norms help deal with the stress due to unpredictability, but then there can be stress if people wonder whether they are following norms in a proper manner or not.

These complexities involving the possibility of stress lead to the observation that there are socially acceptable outlets for stress in high uncertainty avoidant cultures. In everyday terms, there are opportunities for people to "let off steam" in cultures where there are many norms that guide everyday behaviors. And even if people act in a seemingly irresponsible or juvenile manner during these letting-off-steam episodes, there is no damage to their reputations as socially skilled members of their cultures.

Cultures Have Safety Valves for Stress in People's Lives

Having received lots of advice from colleagues who had lived in Asia, Ron Stover finalized his travel arrangements to Seoul, Korea. Ron had accepted a position in the marketing division of a Korean automobile manufacturing company. Originally from California, Ron's colleagues had told him that many Koreans are reserved and formal in the workplace. Further, they told him that close relationships develop slowly and that he should exercise caution with his suggestions about improving marketing policies at the company.

Upon his arrival in Seoul, Ron expected to spend some evenings and weekends by himself. However, after just two weeks he was invited to an evening out with his colleagues. People went to a soccer game, dressed in their favorite team's colors, and cheered and shouted loudly at good and bad plays on the field. After the game, they went to a nightclub where alcohol flowed freely. Ron's immediate boss told jokes and even criticized some recent company decisions. Ron decided that this group of Koreans was very open and informal and that he could start making his suggestions for improvements at work.

Ron may be making a mistake. He is assuming that the same informality and camaraderie expressed during the evening events will also exist in the workplace. He does not realize that in Korean culture, evening socializing and workplace interactions are guided by very different norms. Social events can be informal and raucous, but this does not extend to the workplace. Back at his job in the company, Ron has to realize that behaviors are guided by more formal norms that discourage open expression of personal opinions and emotions.

All cultures have safety valves that allow people to reduce their tensions and to "blow off steam." In the United States, people engage in loud criticism of referees and umpires at sporting events. In Russia, people drink vodka and then share their innermost thoughts, or their "souls." In Japan, people dance in the streets during various community festivals. Some safety valve activities can be dangerous. In their automobiles, Americans use very colorful language while shouting at other drivers and making hand gestures that communicate estimates of the others' intelligence. These activities, however, can keep a driver's attention away from road hazards and careless pedestrians.

Mistakes are made when safety valve behaviors are mistaken for workplace behaviors. In the United States, people know that individuals who attend baseball games and shout at umpires are not necessarily hostile and unpleasant colleagues at work. In Korea, people who tell bawdy jokes and criticize their company during an evening social event will not behave in similar ways during the workday.

UNCERTAINTY AVOIDANCE AND INTERGROUP RELATIONS

A culture's norms can guide many kinds of everyday behaviors. One set of norms limits people's movement in society and consequently can have an impact on people's chances to pursue attractive life opportunities. These are norms that tell people who they should and should not interact with. These norms are especially strong in cultures with a long-standing caste or class system. Interestingly, these norms can weaken if people move from the country where they learned norms that limited intergroup relations.

Culture Affects Interactions Based on Group Memberships

As Human Resources Director of a large engineering firm in Portland, Oregon, Paula Stevens was especially interested in the career development of employees from other countries. She found that with special orientation programs to introduce them to American norms and everyday practices, their adjustment was hastened. On certain issues, however, she needed to say very little since people adjusted very quickly. Many of these issues centered on individual freedoms, such as making one's own choices concerning everyday interpersonal interactions.

Bhola Paswan and Rajesh Sharma were both from the Indian state of Bihar, and they had attended the Indian Institute of Technology in Kanpur. They were very friendly at work, ate lunch together frequently, and brought their families to weekend social events sponsored by the firm. Paula had learned that the two were from different caste groups in India. Rajesh was a Brahman, India's highest caste. Bhola was a Dusad, a caste more commonly referred to as "untouchable" in the United States. Paula asked them to talk about life in India and the United States during one of her orientation sessions.

Bhola and Rajesh agreed that interactions among different caste groups are far easier in the United States. They admitted that their friendship would be next to impossible in India since the caste system is still a force, despite the protests of Mahatma Gandhi and other Indian leaders. In the United States, people are more likely to be judged on the basis of their character and work contributions. Most Americans don't know very much about the caste system, and this works to the advantage of Indian immigrants. Bhola and members of his family can go to work, attend schools, and interact in the general community without the stigma of an imposed status given to them at birth. Rajesh and other Brahmans often point out that they enjoy "loosing the excess baggage" of being forced to limit their interactions with others based on caste status.

There are remnants of the "excess baggage" that may continue to influence behavior. Bhola and Rajesh will probably be uncomfortable if their children start dating. If children of dating age persist, this may force more change within the two families as they make various adjustments to the United States. Children of immigrants have long been major agents of change within families. They want to participate in the activities of their age peers, such as dating and going to school dances, and these may be totally unfamiliar to their parents. They are encouraged to formulate their own opinions by teachers, but this may lead to disagreements with their fathers. Immigrants who had long planned to return to their own countries may stay in the United States because they see more opportunities for their children, or they fear that their children will make a poor adjustment to the country of their parents.

UNCERTAINTY AVOIDANCE AND ETHNOCENTRISM

People spend a great deal of time and energy learning the norms of the culture into which they were born. As has been discussed, these norms guide behaviors in many social situations: eating, working, engaging in social activities, and making choices regarding friendship formations. There is a danger that after people learn the norms of their own culture, they will feel that these should be the norms everywhere. It is difficult to deal with the complex thought, "I learned norms to help obtain goals, people in other cultures might have learned very different behaviors to obtain similar goals, but that is just fine with me." More commonly, people engage in ethnocentric thinking and feel that the way they have learned to behave should be normative everywhere.

Ethnocentrism refers to the belief that one's own cultural group has found correct ways of living and that all other groups should be judged by these standards. The term can be broken down into its components. "Ethno" refers to one's own ethnic or cultural group. "Centrism" means that one's own group should be looked upon as the center of the world. Further, other groups are at a disadvantage because its members do not behave according to proper and reasonable standards.

Examples of standards include beliefs that one's own group practices the correct religion, eats the right foods according to good manners, knows how to treat people well, has discovered the best ways of educating their children, and votes for the most qualified and caring political candidates. When viewing the behavior of individuals from other groups, differences lead to judgments of "incorrect, quaint, or ill-mannered." Ethnocentric people have a solution: members of other groups should adopt the proper standards of behavior long practiced in their more enlightened culture.

When people act in a prejudiced manner, they move beyond judgments of incorrectness and quaintness. They add a strong emotional component so that judgments of other people's behavior become much more negative and much more intense. Judgments of incorrectness become stupidity. Bemused reactions that other people's behaviors are quaint are intensified into conclusions about hopeless backwardness. In its most intense forms, prejudice leads to the decision that the others are so unfortunate that they cannot be helped. If this is their conclusion, then prejudiced people don't interact with members of other groups since they believe it is a waste of their time.

Everyone behaves according to ethnocentric standards of behavior. American business students spend years in college learning about management, marketing, finance, accounting, and computer technology. They have to believe that these are years well spent. Business executives spend years learning about how best to treat employees, and some of their judgments will reflect cultural standards that they learned during their socialization. Ethnocentrism, however, does not inevitably lead to prejudice. People can use one of their greatest gifts: their ability to think carefully about themselves and others. They can learn to observe behavior in other cultures and conclude, "I don't behave that way. But I should not make judgments until I understand how this unfamiliar behavior assists people meet the expectations of *their* culture."

11

Workplace Dynamics

ADJUSTING TO DIFFERING WAYS OF DOING BUSINESS

Most of the intercultural interactions discussed throughout this book deal with people who have tasks to accomplish. For example, businesspeople want to establish joint ventures. Once these are functioning, companies in different countries will often have exchanges of personnel so that employees have opportunities to learn international operations on a firsthand basis. These people will experience the intercultural challenges already discussed: adjusting to other cultures, learning to communicate effectively (Dinsbach et al., 2007), differences in decision-making styles, male-female interactions, and so forth.

Many intercultural interactions will involve workplace dynamics. That is, workers in different countries learn to engage in certain behaviors so that they can complete tasks assigned to them. If they are very good at completing their tasks through means appropriate in their own culture, they become candidates for promotions and for prominence in executives' plans for company expansion. These plans often include international expansion in the acquisition of raw materials, manufacturing, and marketing. In the thinking of executives, the people who are most successful in their own countries become the people who are expected to do well during their assignments in other countries.

A subtle problem often arises. The people who are successful in their own country have mastered appropriate norms for workplace behavior. In fact, they may be quite proud of their reputations for being able to complete tasks in ways that are models for younger and less experienced workers. The fact that they can complete tasks successfully may become part of their positive self-images. But these methods may not be appropriate in other cultures given different workplace norms and dynamics. People on overseas assignments sometimes must unlearn behaviors that lead to success in their own country and must learn a new set of behaviors appropriate in the country to which they are assigned. This is a difficult task since it demands multiple steps (Dunning, Heath, & Suls, 2004). People must have the cultural awareness to know that they should expect differences when assigned to other cultures. They must have the self-insight to know that previously learned behaviors, which led to success in their own country, may have to be modified. This means that they must have the ability to monitor and to think about their own behavior, not a talent possessed by everyone. In addition, people must be willing to invest the time and energy needed to learn previously unfamiliar behaviors that are more appropriate for workplace interactions in other countries.

One of the clearest cultural differences revolves around the scheduling of meetings (Levine, 1997). Is punctuality, as defined by adherence to agreed-upon times marked by clocks and watches, highly valued? Or are previously agreed upon times for scheduled meetings not taken so seriously, with other uses of people's time given priority? When talking with businessmen from North American and Western Europe, stories about disagreements due to punctuality and uses of time are very common.

Arranging the Workday: Clocks and Events

A team of officials from New York City's visitor industry traveled to Brazil and Argentina to explore how tourism from these countries could be increased. Team members had scheduled meeting with government officials, executives in the private sector, and with the directors of major tourist attractions. After returning to New York, team members met to compare experiences and to formulate plans for the future. While there were many differences, one common experience was that scheduled meeting often did not start on time. Meetings scheduled for 1:30 P.M., for example, might not start until 3:00 P.M. or later. The team members complained that it was hard to stay occupied while sitting in reception rooms waiting for meetings to start.

One cultural difference that is helpful in understanding this incident is the distinction between "clock time" and "event time." People everywhere need to arrange activities during their workdays. If they organize these activities by the clock, then various meetings and tasks are scheduled at set times and are often written down on a calendar. In clock time cultures, people become uncomfortable if they have to deviate from their calendars and use terms like, "I'm running late."

In event time cultures, meetings and tasks begin and end according to people's current feelings about time rather than by previously written down schedules. Events take a certain amount of time to complete, and they shouldn't be rushed. After one event is given its proper amount of time, another event can start. The executives who were late for meeting with the visitors from New York were likely finishing up events that began earlier in the workday. A subordinate may have needed last minute advice for a task, a relative may have called about a family matter, or a colleague may have had pictures of a newborn baby that had to be admired. These events demand time and the executives are expected to show respect for people by sharing appropriate amounts of their busy workdays.

How might the visitors from New York have modified their behaviors? They could have started their own events. They could have engaged the executives' assistants in conversations about tourism and about marketing to upscale travelers. They could have admired pictures of the assistants' children. They could have asked for the assistants' recommendations for other influential people who might be contacted. With knowledge of this cultural difference, members of the New York team could be prepared to set aside their clock time cultures and instead could participate in various unfolding events.

INITIAL INTERACTIONS WITH POTENTIAL BUSINESS COLLEAGUES

Businesspeople are wise to make inquiries about how people schedule their days and to learn the importance of punctuality. Of course, the United States is not the only country where meetings are expected to start at an agreed upon time. Businesspeople working in Japan will not have difficulties due to differing expectations about punctuality. However, they may encounter another set of problems if they do not have business cards to exchange with Japanese counterparts whom they meet.

Business Cards Aid Discourse in Japan

Ron Olsen worked in Detroit for a large firm that imported automobile replacement parts. He traveled to Japan with the goal of identifying companies that might enter into joint venture agreements. Fortunately, he learned of an upcoming convention in Nagoya whose attendees worked in the automobile industry. He e-mailed his home office, a Japanese colleague there put him in touch with the convention organizers, and they issued an invitation to Ron.

Ron knew that Japanese businesspeople exchange business cards, and so he had some made while still in Detroit. However, he forgot to take them to the convention. Upon meeting people, they would offer him their cards but he would be unable to reciprocate. Ron was surprised that conference participants seemed to have difficulty communicating with him.

Ron knew of the norm that business cards are exchanged but he underestimated its importance. The Japanese language has various stylistic features that are used with people of different status levels compared to the speaker. There is a style for those with higher status, equal status, and lower status. A company president in Japan would use one style with government officials of equal status, and another style with recent college graduates just starting their careers.

If Ron does not present his business card that gives the name of his organization and his title, then the Japanese have a very difficult time deciding what style to use. Rather than make a mistake, the Japanese might say very little. And, if Japanese businesspeople say little, it is impossible to discuss areas of mutual interest. In contrast to Japanese, English has an important feature that might be called "one style fits all." There is a collection of phrases accompanied by a pleasant voice tone that can be used with many people of varying status levels. In Hawaii for example, regardless of who they are communicating with, people frequently find themselves using phrases such as: "How was your trip? Are you over jet lag yet? Have you had a chance to go to the beach?"

Another implication is that people doing business in Japan frequently engage in title inflation. Salespeople become assistant vice presidents for marketing, and computer specialists become directors of electronic information processing. The belief is that prestigious titles lead to better treatment in Japan. Title inflation is not recommended, however, because the Japanese may overestimate the decision-making powers of the visiting businesspeople and will lose respect if the Americans cannot deliver on promises.

DEVELOPING BUSINESS RELATIONSHIPS

If sojourners are successful in initiating business relationships, they must then worry about developing them beyond polite interactions. In developing serious relationships that could lead to mutually beneficial business dealings, sojourners need to know about differing expectations concerning how businesspeople show seriousness of intent. In some countries, businesspeople exchange gifts to show that they want to develop good relationships. In other countries, large and expensive gifts are illegal.

Gift Giving and Cooperative Business Ventures

"I know that gift giving in Asia is a way of developing business relationships, but I wonder if things have gone too far," Tricia Fernandez said at a weekly staff meeting. Tricia was the sales manger at a large automotive dealership in Tacoma, Washington. She had recently entertained a visit from Kilho Park, who represented the North American marketing division of Hyundai Motors. Traveling from Korea, he first gave Tricia a pen with the Hyundai logo on it. After a combination of both small talk and business discussions, Tricia mentioned that her son had started guitar lessons and that she had seen Korean-made guitars in several music stores. The next day, Kilho came to the dealership with a very nice classical guitar for Tricia's son.

Tricia is correct that gifts are often exchanged in Korea and other Asian countries, and the purpose is to develop or to cement working relationships. For Americans who are the recipients of the gifts, difficulties arise if they feel that a "quid pro quo" exchange is expected. In this example, Tricia can quite reasonably feel that Kilho expects favorable treatment for a proposal he might make concerning Hyundai Motors and the dealership she represents. She might want to return the classical guitar, but this might hurt Kilho's feelings given that he put time and effort into choosing a personal gift.

People in different cultures develop business relationships in various ways. In the United States, people often talk for long periods of time and disclose information about family members, hobbies, and political views. Americans draw from these interpersonal exchanges in making final decisions about joint business ventures. In Korea, people are often very uncomfortable exchanging personal information in the early weeks of relationship development. The presentation of personal gifts becomes a substitute for exchanges of personal information.

One of my colleagues, Min Sun Kim, who is from Seoul, Korea, points out that small and inexpensive gifts provided by one's company cause few difficulties. This means that Korean businesspeople often travel with letter openers, calendars, and paperweights. Problems begin when the company representatives buy expensive personalized gifts based on knowledge learned during business discussions. Dr. Kim once had to discuss returning a rare handmade antique box to a Korean who wanted employment in the United States. She did not know of relevant job openings and so felt uncomfortable accepting an expensive gift.

Continuing with the topic of business relationship development, I would like to discuss an issue for which I do not have advice that will be of use to everyone. The issue is late night socializing in places where alcohol flows freely.

Late Night Socializing Is Expected in Many Countries

Many sojourning businesspeople are uncomfortable with behaviors expected during late night socializing. I have spoken with colleagues from China, Russia, and Japan, and they agree that late night socializing among businesspeople involves a great deal of alcohol consumption. Many Americans are quite health conscious and have cut down on their drinking or have given it up entirely. So can Americans avoid alcohol and still do business in these countries?

Alcohol consumption among businesspeople serves the goal of developing closer relationships. In China, Russia, Japan and some other countries, there are many expectations concerning proper day-to-day behavior, especially for the highest level executives in an organization. People don't talk about personal issues in their lives during the workday, for example, to the degree that Americans do. Restaurants and nightclubs are the accepted places where businesspeople can "let down their hair" and talk about themselves and their personal lives. This sharing of personal information is made easier after people have had a few drinks and feel less inhibited. People feel that they can trust others after everyone has showed their inner selves under the influence of alcohol.

I have tried to develop a list of "substitute behaviors" that will serve the purpose of developing trusting relationships without the health hazards of alcohol. How about modestly priced but carefully selected gifts that are of special interest to potential business partners? These gifts might be appreciated, but they do not contribute to the important step of lowering inhibitions so that inner selves can be displayed. How about karaoke, where people act somewhat silly while stumbling through a song? Yes, this can be part of late night socializing, but alcohol will be served and teetotalers will be noticed!

My colleagues in "expectations of late night socializing" cultures have advice, but it deals with preparations for these events. Businesspeople should talk to others about various nonprescription drugs and health food store items they might take to lessen the effects of alcohol and to soften the inevitable hangovers. If they travel in a group, they might decide that one of the younger people should drink less so that someone can monitor business negotiations the next day. They can try to identify individual businesspeople in these countries who have learned to dislike frequent late night carousing. In addition, they can continue the perhaps elusive search for various "substitute behaviors."

UNDERSTANDING ORGANIZATIONAL STRUCTURES IN WHICH PEOPLE MUST WORK

In many countries, the development of business relationships is essential to getting anything done. In such countries, there are not well established government offices and chambers of commerce that can assist visiting people who have not yet established a set of interpersonal relationships. In the absence of such institutions, businesspeople who have developed good relationships trade favors and help each other with the paperwork, rules, and regulations that are inevitable parts of doing international business (Luo & Chen, 1996; Wang et al., 2000).

Bureaucracies Have Their Attractions

Chu Jin, from Beijing, had traveled to Boston for the purpose of examining joint venture possibilities in the manufacturing of component parts for computers. His counterpart in Boston was Jim Allen. About a month into his stay, Chu Jin found that he needed some paperwork to complete a report that he wanted to send back to his home office in Beijing. He needed one tax form for claims on depreciation of inventory, and he also needed application forms for English as a second language classes at a local public school.

Chu Jin asked Jim if he knew some people who could get these forms for him. Jim said, "No, but I can call the tax office and the local school and talk to people who can send these materials to you." Jim got on the phone, made two calls, and fifteen minutes later said that the tax and school forms should be in the mail by the end of the workday. Chu Jin looked stunned and did not know how to respond to Jim's news.

The cultural difference is that in China, people obtain information and official paperwork through their personal connections or through the connections of others whom they know. These connections are called one's "guanxi." People spend large amounts of time nurturing their guanxi, and those without it have a very difficult time achieving their goals. In the United States, people have insisted on a responsive bureaucracy whose employees are expected to be efficient in the distribution of basic information and paperwork. Americans do not have to know the person at the other end of the phone when they make a request. If the person in the bureaucracy is responsible for dispensing information and paperwork, then this is likely to happen.

I once asked a colleague from Shanghai how she would contact a government official for a basic tax form. She replied, "I wouldn't even try. I would have to ask around and find a friend who knows the government official."

Business people who are aware of this difference between countries recommend that long-term Chinese visitors be introduced and integrated into a supportive group after they arrive in the United States. Even though these visitors could get on the phone and obtain information and various documents, they are more comfortable doing this through interactions with people they know rather than with strangers in an unseen bureaucracy.

Of course, behaviors have to change if Americans travel to China. If Jim Allen from this incident was working in China, he would have to accomplish his goals through a set of personal contacts whose creation would take a great deal of time and energy. There is an interesting result of such international experiences. Americans become more patient and even appreciative of bureaucracies once they return to their own country.

Some countries, then, do not have well-established bureaucratic systems. People achieve workplace goals through interpersonal contacts that take a great deal of time to develop. If these contacts are high status people who have a great deal of clout, so much the better. In attempts to develop a set of interpersonal contacts, people in companies seeking international expansion will try to nurture relationships with individuals from other countries. These efforts can take the form of hosting sojourners from highly industrialized nations. Problems can arise, as in this incident.

Overseas Assignments: Window Dressing or Serious Work?

Since his eventual goal was a career in international business, George Kagawa accepted a position in a large electronics company in Osaka, Japan, after graduating from college. Originally from Honolulu, George was a third-generation Japanese American. At college, he took four years of Japanese language and enrolled for every elective course in Japanese Studies and International Business. Upon arrival in Osaka, he met his immediate supervisor, Kazuo Nishimura. Soon, George began to have difficulties. It seemed that Mr. Nishimura was not familiar with George's background. He was not given job assignments consistent with his extensive background in computer science. In fact, he found himself staring out the window given that he had so little to do.

George has encountered a set of problems that some Americans face when accepting jobs in Japan. These difficulties do not always occur, but they happen frequently enough so that Americans should be prepared. In some Japanese companies, it is seen as prestigious to have Americans as employees. It communicates to others, "See how international we are becoming." Given that English has become the language of international business, it is useful to have some native-English speakers on the payroll so that they can act as informal translators when clients from other countries visit. George may be asked to do some translation at meetings, but he may be very uncomfortable given a lack of experience with this difficult task.

The danger is that Americans are treated as "window dressing" or accessories and are not invited to important meetings, are not given responsible assignments, and are not integrated into workgroups. If they are prepared for these possibilities, Americans can take some steps. They can take the initiative and find meaningful tasks themselves. Some Americans start English language classes, and these often prove very popular since many Japanese want to improve their English and value opportunities to interact with native speakers. In return, Japanese coworkers will sometimes make attempts to integrate the Americans into workgroups within the company.

Career counselors familiar with this potential problem advise sojourners to look at job assignments in Japan as an important step in career development. However, they add that if people wait for good things to happen, the assignment may not be a good career investment. People should seek opportunities to improve their Japanese, identify and follow through with efforts to make contributions in the company, and join voluntary organizations outside the company that will lead to skill development. By taking these steps, people can sometimes build up enough goodwill that their proposals for responsible workplace projects will be taken seriously.

DECIDING ON A WORKPLACE COMMUNICATION STYLE

In previous chapters, communication styles and decision making were discussed. I would like to review a few key points and apply them to difficult work situations. In my work in Hawaii, working with many students from Asia and many students whose parents and grandparents are from Asian countries, I frequently find myself discussing a soft and quiet versus a dynamic and forceful communication style. Sometimes one approach is more effective, and sometimes the other helps people meet goals. The skills sojourners need to develop include the ability to use both styles and to identify the work situations where each is effective. At times, people might prefer one style but will be more effective if the other is used. Both of the following incidents took place in Hawaii, and they are based on my personal experiences.

A Quiet Approach during Meetings Can Serve People's Goals

"This should be a good session at the conference," Kathy Chun told other members of the planning committee. Kathy and her colleagues were finalizing plans for various sessions at the Hawaii Conference for Human Resource Professionals. The meetings were to extend over three days. For the first day, Kathy had received a commitment from Frank Weldon, who was flying in from California for the conference. Frank had a reputation as a dynamic speaker who could present challenging ideas that encouraged creative thinking among audience members.

Previously, Frank had called Kathy to find out as much as possible about conference attendees. Kathy told him that people would come from many backgrounds, given Hawaii's cultural diversity, and that some attendees would be from various Asian countries. Frank mentioned that he had traveled to Asia several times over the last five years. He said that he would be happy to work with Kathy on this presentation the first day, and he reminded her that he would also be speaking on the conference's last day.

After Frank's presentation the first day, Kathy was disappointed. While not a total bore, Frank's talk was not particularly dynamic and many of the ideas he covered were already familiar to audience members. Kathy wondered why Frank had not lived up to his reputation.

Frank may be behaving in a quiet, reserved manner while learning about conference attendees and deciding how he can present his ideas most effectively. Frank has been in Asia and knows that presenters often speak in a less dynamic style than is common in the United States. He also knows that disagreements are taken very seriously. If some of his audience members have taken public positions opposite to Frank's, these people might have difficulty interacting effectively with him during the rest of the conference (Foa & Chemers, 1967). Frank may feel that it is best to be noncontroversial early in the program and to use the first two days to discover people's range of opinions on different issues. Then, at his second presentation, he can present his ideas while at the same time recognizing and showing respect for the positions held by others.

I've seen this approach work effectively in Hawaii. If people give their firm ideas too quickly, they can be dismissed as know-it-all loudmouths. If a committee is to have meetings over several months, it is often best to be reserved during the first four or five weeks. People can learn what their colleague's positions are, can think about their own positions, and can later offer suggestions that integrate the strengths of various ideas. Good advice for meeting organizers is to be patient. If early sessions seem tame and uneventful, various people may be using the "wait and then contribute" approach. Future meetings are likely to be much more dynamic.

So the soft style is more effective in this work situation involving an outsider who wanted to integrate his ideas with those of others. In the following incident, the social situation calls for a more dynamic and forceful style, and people who do not use it will put themselves at a disadvantage.

A Modest Communication Style May Not Work during Job Interviews

Stan Tsai, from Hawaii, had recently graduated with honors from UCLA. He began interviewing for jobs in Honolulu. At one organization, a member of the interview panel asked Stan about winning the Dean's academic award. Stan replied in a shy and timid manner, "My parents encouraged me to work hard at my studies." Another panel member asked him about a prestigious club and his election as president. Stan replied,

"It was nice of the other students to give me the chance." After the interview, panel members commented to each other that they wished Stan had been more dynamic when discussing his academic record and job qualifications.

Stan is using a modest and self-effacing presentation style that is common in Hawaii. The style has its origins in Asia where people are socialized to call attention to others rather than to themselves. In his first response, Stan made reference to his parents and he showed his respect for them by diverting attention from himself. In his second response, he showed gratitude to his fellow students for giving him a chance to be president of the club. Calling attention to oneself, using a dynamic tone of voice, can be seen as boastful and self-promoting.

Many young professionals from Hawaii want to live in their home state if they can find suitable jobs. Another reason for modest self-presentation is that, as part of their socialization, adolescents are told not to "make A." This term, known by virtually all locals, refers to avoiding embarrassing activities that would make a person look like a jerk. People cut down the chances of "making A" if they develop a modest and quiet communication style. If locals avoid embarrassing events, they cannot be reminded of these when they see old classmates at one of Hawaii's shopping centers. On the mainland United States, people often move from the communities where they grew up. If they made embarrassing mistakes, and learned from them, they don't necessarily encounter people who remember these clumsy errors.

Executives in Hawaii familiar with the potential problem of modest styles recommend that other methods for selecting among applicants be used in addition to interviews. For example, people knowing they will be entering the job market can seek internships. In such positions, they can demonstrate their knowledge and skills over a longer period of time than the one hour allotted for a job interview.

There is a dilemma for individual job seekers. They can hope that companies will have policies that allow other methods besides interviews to be used during the selection process. Or, they can practice a more forceful approach to their self-presentation communications. I recommend the latter, because job seekers will not always find companies with several methods of selection.

My further recommendation is that people learn both the soft and forceful styles and learn to use them in different social situations. How do they decide? People can think through the situations where they will be interacting and can ask questions such as the following. What are my goals? What are the goals of the people with whom I will be interacting? Am I an outsider or am I a familiar insider? What style of interaction do others expect? If I am forceful, will I be seen as a loudmouth or will I be seen as a self-confident potential employee? If I am soft, will I be seen as respectfully modest or will I be seen as an ineffective wimp? From my talks with others who have had a great deal of experience in different social situations, which style will lead to the accomplishment of my goals and those of others?

If people go through an exercise involving asking and answering questions like these, they should be able to make good decisions concerning the choice of a communication style.

12

Developing Interpersonal Relationships

THE IMPORTANCE OF OTHER PEOPLE

Toward the end of one of his movies, Woody Allen told a joke about a man who visited a psychiatrist. The man told the psychiatrist that he had a friend who thought he was a chicken. This friend was a very popular individual who had good relationships with many people. But his belief that he was a chicken was causing problems, such as the need to find restaurants that served raw corn seeds when he went out with friends. The psychiatrist told the man, "I think I can help him if you can encourage him to come and see me. I think I can help him come to grips with the fact that he is a person and not a chicken." The man then said, "But we need the eggs." Then, during one of the few occasions where he explained a joke, Woody Allen said, "That's what it is about relationships. We need the eggs."

People need others in their lives. Very few of us would be happy living as hermits. People provide various types of resources: companionship, information, nurturance, affection, favors, services, and so forth (Zimbardo & Lieppe, 1991). Of course, relationships can go foul and can cause distress. Almost everyone can think of a person that they once knew and to whom they felt close, but they no longer feel this way. In addition, they can think of the exact reasons, such as the betrayal of confidences or the refusal to repay debts.

Some relationships go wrong because the people involved define them differently. One person may think that a certain relationship is very close, but the other person thinks that it is a casual working relationship. This can be especially true when people come from different cultural backgrounds and have different definitions of terms such as "cousin," "friend," "colleague," and "neighbor."

One way to think about relationships is to examine the amount of emotional closeness among people. People can think about individuals who are very close to them. They spend a great deal of free time together. The emotions that are experienced by one person are felt by the other person. If one person in the relationship has a problem, the other person would be insulted if no request for help was made. What's a good term for these people? "Close family members and long-time friends" is one phrase that captures people who have these strong bonds.

People can then think of individuals who are not as close as members of this first group. Every emotional up and down is not shared. But the people socialize with each other and enjoy getting together once in a while. These people stop and chat with each other if they unexpectedly see each other at a shopping mall. These people might be invited to a big wedding involving three hundred or more guests, but would probably not be invited to a small wedding with thirty guests. There are different terms for these individuals. Americans frequently use the word "friends," and some people use a term such as "acquaintances."

Then there is a third grouping. These people do not socialize together frequently. They would not be insulted if they were not invited to big weddings. But the people are on a first-name basis and talk with each other when they are at the same social gatherings, such as political fund-raisers or receptions for a company's new vice president. These people feel free to call each other on the phone when they need favors in the form of information or professional referrals. They trade favors, and ideally maintain a balance of benefits given and received so that they do not develop the reputation of being users and takers. A commonly used term to describe these people is that they are members of each other's network.

Problems can arise when one person feels that there is one type of relationship but another person disagrees. Americans, for example, frequently offer enthusiastic welcomes to visitors from other countries. They add phrases such as, "You must drop by our house some time." If the newcomers take this invitation literally, they can be extremely disappointed if they learn that the Americans were very casual with their remark and did not expect a visit.

Good interpersonal relationships are important for all people, and sojourners are no exception (Bochner, 2006; Mak & Buckingham, 2007;

Uskul, Hynie, & Lanonde, 2004; Yoshida, 1994). Sojourners often find that they need relationships with host nationals to solve problems: discovering workplace rules, interpreting communications from superiors, finding schools for their children and apartments where they will live, expanding one's business contacts, identifying leisure time activities, and so forth. In this chapter, relationship development will be discussed. Discussion will start with initial interactions as people meet for the first time, the nurturing of relationships, and the maturing of relationships as people identify each other as close friends or colleagues.

MEETING OTHERS FOR THE FIRST TIME

As with so many examples in the analysis of people's experiences as they move from one culture to another, behaviors during initial interactions carry different meanings for the individuals involved.

Initial Interactions: Superficial or Sincere Behaviors

After a month in Cleveland, Vu Nguyen began to feel comfortable going to business meetings where he knew few, if any, people. Originally from Hanoi, Vu had accepted an assignment to develop American markets for a factory that produced textiles with high quality detailed patterns. At one meeting, he met Dan Barry, an executive with an interior design company. Dan told Vu that he was happy to meet him and that he looked forward to future interactions. About three weeks later, Vu happened to see Dan during intermission at a concert both were attending. Vu greeted Dan, but Dan did not seem to recognize him. Vu thought to himself, "Superficial American, just as I had been warned!"

The complaint that Americans are superficial in their interactions with international visitors is common. On college campuses, teachers of English as a second language comment that "superficial" is one of the first four-syllable words that students from Asia use in their everyday conversations. The complaint stems from a cultural difference. In Asia, most people are members of a collective that has a very strong influence in their lives. This collective is often the extended family, and it can also include the company for which one works. There are benefits to collective membership such as social support (Glazer, 2006) in times of crisis, but there are also extensive obligations to help other members. Given these benefits and obligations, joining a collective as an adult is a major commitment.

In the United States, people are socialized to view themselves as individuals rather than as members of a permanent group with lifetime obligations (as discussed in Chapter 3). They move in and out of interactions as a way of achieving their goals. This leads to the development of certain social skills, such as meeting people quickly in a cheery and pleasant manner, putting them at their ease, and using remarks such as, "I hope we talk again soon!" When people from collective cultures hear such remarks, they take them very seriously and feel that a close relationship has been offered. When they find out that the Americans were not offering friendship, they become disappointed.

Visitors from collectivist countries should view initial meetings with Americans as offering the possibility but not the certainty of continued interactions. Americans should realize that these interactions are taken seriously. They should make attempts to remember names and faces and to appreciate the signals that their behavior sends.

In the business world, people need to know many different individuals with whom they can trade favors in the form of exchanged pieces of information, referrals, and introductions to others so that any one person's network increases. The way this process of meeting others is done differs across cultures.

Receptions: Interactions with Many or Few People?

"My feet feel as if they are stuck in cement," Wang Jin said to himself as he observed people circulating smoothly at a reception to which he had been invited. Wang Jin, from Nanjing, China, had traveled to Seattle, Washington, to represent a company that produced fine dinnerware. He had no difficulties identifying potential buyers at upscale stores. One day, he was invited to a reception for the new vice president of a large department store. The reception started at 7:00 P.M., and Wang Jin arrived just a few minutes late. As the evening progressed, he noticed that people spent a few minutes with many different people, moving from individual to individual in a seemingly effortless manner. Wan Jin tried to talk with others and even though people were friendly, he was very uncomfortable integrating himself into the movement from person to person.

When I ask businesspeople from Asia about difficulties adjusting to the United States, they say it is hard to attend receptions where they are expected to circulate. In China, Wang Jin would have attended many receptions, but interactions among people are different. People often spend the evening with others whom they already know. They might meet one or two people for the first time, but these would be based on introductions from high status individuals who feel that certain people should become acquainted. Receptions often take the form of banquets where people share the same table for an evening and are not expected to interact with people at other tables.

Chinese businesspeople are able to give advice, some of it humorous, to Americans who are invited to social gatherings in China. They advise people to arrive at the party early and to look for individuals who are having an animated discussion. "Be sure the group you join has some interesting people, because you will be with them all evening." Older and high status people often arrive late and younger guests are expected to give them attention and deference. "If you want to avoid interacting with the older executives, try to maneuver your group into a corner so that you will have the excuse of not seeing people who arrive late."

Americans who know this cultural difference can offer assistance. At the reception in Seattle, someone might "rescue" Wang Jin and introduce him to others. Wang Jin is likely to be highly appreciative and may return the favor with various concessions during upcoming business negotiations.

When sojourners arrive in a country, others who are concerned with their adjustment often invite them to various types of social gatherings. The exact type of social gathering may be unfamiliar to the sojourners, and so they should be careful what they say upon receiving invitations. If they make mistakes, they may face social rejection. The rejection is not due to hosts' prejudices but rather to the inappropriate behavior of sojourners.

Factors Other than Prejudice Affect Intercultural Interactions

"Baby luau! What's that?" Jack Lynch asked his coworker, Kimo Keala. Jack arrived in Honolulu two months ago and was employed by a construction company. He had worked on a variety of building projects in Nevada and often made suggestions to coworkers in Hawaii concerning ways to improve their efficiency. After Kimo explained what a baby luau was, Jack declined the invitation since he did not think it would be an interesting way to use his free time. After turning down the invitation, Jack felt that people at work were beginning to ignore him, especially his suggestions for improvements. He concluded, "I guess there is more prejudice in Hawaii against mainlanders than locals want to admit."

Jack is undoubtedly experiencing some rejection, but he may not be diagnosing it accurately. "Prejudice" can be examined by breaking the word into component parts. Prejudice refers to judgments made before complex and extensive information is carefully considered (Hamilton & Hewstone, 2007). Most often, the term is used when referring to groups of people who differ in visible ways. In today's fast-moving workplaces, individuals are extremely busy and encounter many pieces of information that might be used in their everyday decision-making. One set of decisions deals with the question, "Who will we socialize with during our free time in and outside the workplace?"

Often, people from ethnic groups other than one's own are absent from this "social time" list. When looking for explanations (Ross, 1977), skin color and other visible aspects of ethnicity "pull" judgments about why people don't interact in a friendly manner. People then make the easy jump in their thinking from skin color to the judgment that prejudice is rampant.

In Jack's case, his interpersonal difficulties may have little to do with his skin color or ethnicity. Jack has made some cultural errors that can be causing problems. Baby luaus are important events and should be taken very seriously by people fortunate enough to be invited. Long-term residents of Hawaii don't always enjoy the suggestions of newcomers concerning how they should do their jobs. Newcomers should "pay their dues," work hard, and demonstrate their contributions, and wait to be asked for suggestions on how the workplace can be improved.

Rather than immediately concluding that there is ethnic prejudice when people are not interacting in a cordial manner, my advice is to consider culturally influenced behaviors. Hosts can prepare themselves to explain appropriate workplace and after-hours behaviors. Sojourners should be willing to modify habitual behaviors to meet hosts' cultural expectations.

MOVING BEYOND POLITENESS IN INTERPERSONAL RELATIONSHIP DEVELOPMENT

If cultural differences surrounding initial interactions can be surmounted, people may be able to develop strong interpersonal relationships. But as the old song says, it takes "two to tango." In intercultural relationships, problems arise when one person feels that there is a deep interpersonal relationship but the other person feels that the relationship is much more casual.

Americans Use the Word "Friend" for Large Numbers of People

After six months working in Boston, Massachusetts, Derek Hamilton began having lunch with a group of four coworkers. Originally from Leeds, England, Derek worked as a quality control officer in a food manufacturing plant. When his lunch companions asked him how he was enjoying Boston, Derek answered, "I haven't enjoyed it very much yet. It's been hard, for example, to make new friends." One of his American colleagues responded, "What do you mean? We're your friends! We interact frequently at work and get along fine." The other Americans were also upset that Derek did not consider them friends, and interactions at work were chilly for a few weeks.

Derek and his American colleagues have encountered a cultural difference in people's attitudes toward the word "friend." In the United States, the word is used very freely and it includes people who are emotionally close as well as casual acquaintances and workplace colleagues. I remember talking with an American who referred to "a dear friend." Later in the conversation, it became clear that the American had not seen this person for ten years and did now know where in the world he was living.

People from Great Britain are more likely to use the term "friend" for a smaller number of people who are emotionally very close. In addition, these people are likely to spend free time with each other and to share similar interests that lead to shared activities. Working together with people and having cordial relations at work is not enough. People in the workplace can be valued colleagues, but without strong emotional ties and shared leisure time activities the term "friend" is inappropriate for the British.

At an organization I once worked for, an Englishman joined the staff as a senior researcher. After a few months, one of my colleagues invited him to dinner at his house. The Englishman politely declined, and my colleague complained, "He is willing to work with us but not to socialize with us!" As with the previous example, differences in attitudes toward "friendship" come into play. From the Englishman's perspective, it is difficult to form a friendship after only a few months. Further, the British often have the attitude that "People's homes are their castles." They may be uncomfortable visiting the homes of casual acquaintances, feeling that they are invading their privacy.

This cultural difference is one that requires an understanding of cultural differences and mutual adjustment. If they are living in Great Britain, Americans should expect friendships to develop more slowly. If they are living in the United States, British people should accept more social invitations even if they feel that they don't know the Americans very well.

In the following incident, we return to misunderstanding brought on by differences common in individualistic and collectivist cultures (Triandis, 1995). One of the people thought that a close interpersonal relationship had been developed and so small difficulties would be overlooked. A tolerance for small imperfections is crucial for successful relationships. The other person who was a part of the interaction did not look at the relationship in the same way.

Personal Relationships Can Take Second Place to Contracts

Frank Williams and his family had saved for a vacation in Kathmandu, Nepal, for over two years. Family members decided to book with a company that offered a packaged tour led by Pearl Bryan. Traveling from Los Angeles, group members arrived in Kathmandu late one evening, passed through customs, settled into their rooms, and started out the next day on a sightseeing trip in and around the city.

Many of the activities involved ground transportation on a tour bus owned by Suresh Shrestha. As a "hands on" manager, Suresh often talked with tour group members to make sure that their needs were met. He found that Frank and Pearl were especially interested in the history of

Nepal, and he was happy to teach them as much as he could by pointing out important historical sites. The tour was going well, highlighted by a trip to Chitwan National Park to observe elephants, and shopping tours to "Freak Street" in Thamal. One evening, Suresh picked up Pearl and Frank in his car and took them to the site of recent prodemocracy demonstrations.

The next morning, the tour was supposed to leave the hotel at 8:00 A.M. for a trip to a staging area for expeditions to Mount Everest. The bus was late, and it still had not arrived at 9:15 A.M. Frank and Pearl complained to Suresh. Suresh replied that the bus driver might have overslept but that he would be at the hotel soon. Frank and Pearl became visibly upset and pointed to a piece of paper that specified the 8:00 A.M. departure time. Suresh was surprised with the Americans' firm tone of voice and felt betrayed given the positive relationship he had developed with Frank and Pearl.

When problems arise in business dealings, different cultures offer various ways of finding a solution. Suresh brings a relational orientation. He feels that he has developed good personal relations with the Americans, and that difficulties can be handled if people call upon past positive interactions. Americans often bring a more rational orientation to problem solving. "We had an agreement, here it is in writing, and so the bus should be here by now!" People's appeal to the very familiar behaviors of their own culture are more frequent when they are upset and when they feel that their time and money are being wasted.

The relational orientation is common in cultures such as Nepal where people view themselves as long-term members of permanent groups. The rational orientation is common in cultures such as the United States where people depend upon a strong legal system to protect their individual rights.

In collectivist cultures, the development of interpersonal relationships can lead to behaviors that are reserved for in-group members. Sojourners, then, may be treated as members of an in-group without knowing that they have been given this membership. Further, they may miss the fact that in-group membership has both benefits and obligations.

THE OFFER OF IN-GROUP MEMBERSHIP
HAS CONSEQUENCES

Having studied Greek history and architecture in college, Ray Fielding found it easy to have conversations with coworkers in Athens. Ray worked as a market analyst for an import-export company that specialized in men's fashions. Originally from El Paso, Texas, Ray found Athens a very stimulating place to live and work. He became especially close to Dimitri Nassiakou, who worked in the company's accounting department. Dimitri had studied English in college but felt that his knowledge of textbook grammar was better than his knowledge of conversational English. He asked Ray to have conversations with him in English. In exchange, Dimitri helped Ray with basic Greek vocabulary and phrases useful in everyday exchanges with people.

After a few months, Dimitri asked Ray if he wanted to visit the village where he was born and raised. Ray agreed, and they drove to the village, approximately 150 miles from Athens. Many of Dimitri's extended family members welcomed Ray to the village and to their homes. Very quickly, conversations turned to inquiries about Ray's life, and questions became very personal. People asked Ray about his salary, his religion, whether or not he had a girlfriend, and what his political affiliations were. Dimitri's uncle asked Ray whether he wanted to meet some eligible Greek women. Ray became very uncomfortable with these personal questions and had a difficult time keeping up his end of conversations.

Ray has encountered a cultural practice found in Greece and other Mediterranean countries. The starting point for understanding this cultural practice is the distinction between in-groups and out-groups (Brewer, 2007). Everyone has these two types of groups in their lives. In-groups consist of people close to us, who we look forward to being with, and with whom we exchange personal information. Out-groups consist of strangers, people we avoid, and people we rarely talk to because of nonoverlapping interests and attitudes. In Greece, certain people are offered in-group membership very quickly. If people offer help to someone, as Ray did with his English lessons for Dimitri, they show their goodwill and cooperative attitude. Dimitri is certain to have shared information about Ray with his extended family. Consequently, Ray is viewed as "one of us" and will be offered in-group membership. But group membership always carries obligations. In Greece, in-group membership means exchanging a great deal of personal information.

Ray can expect tremendous hospitality from Dimitri's family. He will be offered many meals, will be escorted to various historical sites, and will be met with the reaction of "unthinkable" when he suggests that he stay at a hotel. But there will come a time when favors must be returned, as with any in-group membership. For example, people will know where Ray went to college, and he may be asked to help one of Dimitri's cousins gain admission to that college.

MISUNDERSTANDINGS WHEN ALL PARTIES FEEL THERE IS A CLOSE RELATIONSHIP

Some especially troublesome problems can arise when all parties involved in intercultural interactions feel that they have close ties, friendships, and effective collegial relationships. There are cultural differences surrounding the expectations and obligations of close relationships. People socialized in one culture may have the reputation of knowing how to be "good friends," but they may make mistakes in other cultures where different expectations exist.

Don't Always Expect a Direct "Thank You" for Help Offered

"I hear that you're playing golf with the boss this afternoon," Daryl Nakata said to Steve Baxter as they shared a coffee break at the insurance company in Honolulu where they worked. Daryl had spent his entire life in Hawaii, and Steve had recently moved from the company's large branch in Los Angeles. Daryl had become frustrated with the cumbersome system for travel reimbursements at the company. Employees often had to charge trips on their own credit cards and wait up to three months for repayments. He developed a software program that he felt would streamline the reimbursement process.

Daryl had never felt close to the company president, but he noticed that Steve had a good relationship given a shared interest in golf. He asked Steve to mention travel reimbursements and the new software during the golf match. Steve did so, the president seemed intrigued, and he directed that the accounting department try out the software. Steve thought that he would receive an enthusiastic "thank you" from Daryl, but this did not happen.

The culture in which people are socialized offers them guidance for many everyday behaviors. In Hawaii, there is a mix of behaviors given Asian, Polynesian, and American influences. In the case of direct thanks for help, there are "old school" and "new school" behaviors. If Daryl is behaving according to the old school still common in Asia, a direct "thank you" is not expected. People who have good relationships, as Steve and Daryl seem to in this incident, know that help is appreciated and so direct thanks are unnecessary. Further, if people demonstrate enthusiasm when saying "thank you," this is the sort of public display of emotion that is not encouraged (Wilkins & Gareis, 2006; Yoo, Matsumoto, LeRoux, & Liu, 2006). The "new school" standards, expected among people socialized on the mainland United States, are that direct thanks should be offered quickly and with enthusiasm. Teenagers are given etiquette books for their birthdays to remind them of the social skills their parents have been trying to instill.

Before becoming upset, Steve should consider these old school and new school possibilities. If old school, there can be acknowledgement of the help, but it may come in a substitute form. Steve may find apple bananas from Daryl's backyard on his desk in a few weeks. I once assisted a police officer, now a lieutenant, at a community meeting we both attended. He did not offer a direct "thank you," but he engaged in other behaviors that took much more time. He walked me to my car after the meeting. He laughed at my not-very-funny jokes. Later, he dropped some papayas off at my house. These substitute behaviors that take the place of a direct "thank you" are common in Hawaii and other cultures where people do not feel that they constantly have to acknowledge the help of friends.

Sometimes, people feel that they know the expectations surrounding close relationships. They have read some books, they have talked to others who have had intercultural interactions in the same country, and they have their own personal experiences from which they learned. But they still miss some subtle points.

Cultural Values Combine with Individual Differences in the Workplace

"I thought I understood the cultural emphasis on harmony and cooperation," Jack Parker wrote to friends from his home in Nagoya, Japan. But I don't always see it." Jack was originally from Phoenix, Arizona, and had accepted a three-year assignment in Nagoya. He continued, "Two of my colleagues, for instance, are very quick to criticize others and do not seem to care about hurting their feelings. At the same time, others follow what I thought was an important part of Japanese culture: to be very sensitive to the opinions and feelings of others. All of these people are effective workers, and I can't figure out how they all can be successful in the company I work for."

Jack has encountered a complex aspect of culture's guidance on everyday behaviors. First, he has to keep in mind that the Japanese emphasis on politeness and harmony is focused on some but not all people. The focus is on people "in-between" those who are total strangers, and those with whom one has close and long-term relations. These in-between people include coworkers who are not close colleagues, visitors referred by long-time friends, old school chums who one sees a few times a year, and people who might become long-term customers and clients.

For people who are very close, different Japanese bring varying styles of interpersonal interaction. In other words, they add their individual differences to the cultural guidance learned during their socialization in Japan. Some people maintain a harmonious and soft interpersonal style with those who are close. Jack referred to some of these people in his letter. Other Japanese drop the emphasis on harmony and become much more direct, critical, and demanding. They draw from another aspect of Japanese culture: once group ties are formed, they are permanent. The group becomes a large and unmovable rock, and people don't spend time and energy maintaining rocks. Rather, the presence of rocks is taken for granted, as are long-term relationships among some Japanese. Jack, then, has reached an important point in his Japanese sojourn. Japanese colleagues may start out interactions with Jack by being soft and indirect. If they switch to interactions where they disagree and argue with Jack, this may be a sign that he is becoming accepted as a close workplace colleague.

The difference between a harmonious style and a more direct and critical style is often based on interactions with family members. Some Japanese parents try to instill a harmonious style that extends to interactions among all family members, including themselves. They are not always successful, but if they are, then the children of these families will likely bring a cooperative and sensitive style to their eventual workplaces.

Other parents tolerate teenage loudness, rudeness, and rebelliousness similar to that found in urban areas all over the world. This tolerance extends only to family members: interactions with others (teachers, visitors, salespeople) are expected to be unfailingly polite. But if Japanese teenagers become accustomed to this less-than-harmonious style among those close to them, they may bring this approach to their interactions with long-term colleagues at work.

13

Basic Psychological Processes at Work during Intercultural Interactions

INTRODUCTION: ORGANIZING COMPLEX INFORMATION

The goal of this chapter is to review some basic psychological processes related to information gathering and information processing and to examine how they are applied in the types of intercultural encounters covered throughout this book. One of the basic assumptions is that people use the same psychological processes during intercultural interactions as during their interactions with individuals in their own cultures. However, difficulties and mistakes associated with these psychological processes are intensified during intercultural interactions because of unfamiliarity, lack of preparatory experiences, and the absence of supportive others who can give feedback on the quality of people's interactions.

Many psychological processes are designed to identify and to deal with important information to which people must react. The amount of information to which people are exposed everyday is vast. Advertisers want our attention and want to present information about their products. Friends want us to try new foods by going to lunch at a new ethnic restaurant. Professors want us to give special attention to the material they are presenting, sometimes forgetting that equally competent professors from other departments want the same amount of attention for their material. Bosses want to tell us about the new projects they have in mind. Our children want to read to us to demonstrate the skills they are learning in school. Politicians want us to support some public policies and to give short shrift to others. Civil servants want us to know about current laws regarding driving on freeways, keeping buildings safe from fire hazards, and what new taxes we have to pay.

To deal with this vast amount of information, people have to use the psychological process of categorization. That is, they have to be able to react to individual pieces of information by putting them into categories, and then responding to the category rather than to the individual bit of information. When driving to work, for example, people cannot react to each individual car they see. They can't process information about each blue Honda, each red Ford, and each silver Toyota. Instead they have to form categories: cars going in my direction that are close to me, cars going in the same direction but that are far away, and cars going in the other direction that are directly across the median divide. By reacting to these categories of cars, they can decide how to drive safely to work without being overwhelmed by individual pieces of information represented by specific cars. When they listen to politicians, people can respond to specific campaign promises by using categories such as "policies consistent with my values" and "policies that I think are unwise."

Once people have well-developed categories, they can react efficiently to specific bits of information. When they see one of the hundred of advertisements to which they are exposed daily, they can react efficiently if they have categories such as "products that I use regularly, products that I never use, companies that I trust, companies that have cheated me," and so forth.

So people categorize constantly to deal with the vast amount of information to which they are exposed. Intercultural interactions and sojourns in other countries provide special challenges. People find that the categories with which they are familiar in their own culture are different in other cultures. The foods that are part of people's category of "what I like to eat" provide a good example. In their own culture, people may be familiar with a big piece of meat, a potato, and some vegetables. In other cultures, or in a restaurant to which a friend invites them, they may not find this familiar category. They may be faced with choices among octopus, rice, seaweed, bat, and fertilized eggs where the fetus of a chicken can clearly be seen. While they might get though a meal with these choices in a socially skilled manner, they have many other challenges to their previous categories. For people engaging in intercultural interactions both within their own country and in others, these include appropriate topics of conversation, ways of developing friendships, and interactions with others using an acceptable communication style (Chapters 4 and 5). For people accepting assignments in other countries, the challenges include discovering and filling other categories that summarize important information. Examples are the best ways of getting to work, good schools for the children, interaction styles with bosses, enjoyable leisure time activities, and so forth.

STEREOTYPES

Some categories deal with people. Different individuals are put into a category, the category is given a label, and then people are treated as a category member. Most often, these categories emphasize ethnic group markers such as skin color, facial features such as eye shape, and language or accent when using a certain language.

When categories deal with people, they are often called stereotypes (Risen, Glovich, & Dunning, 2007). At times, use of such categories or stereotypes is necessary. If people are involved in a mugging or robbery, police will ask them about the race or the ethnicity of the criminal. In my teaching, I need to be able to look at my class and decide who is willing to speak up and who will be uncomfortable if I call on them that it will interfere with their learning (Chapter 11). The difference is often based on whether students were raised in collectivistic or in an individualistic culture (Chapter 3). I also have to be prepared for exceptions, for example, students from collectivistic cultures who are very comfortable when they call attention to themselves during classroom discussions.

Often, people resent being put into a stereotyped category because they feel that their individuality is denied and that they are being treated as an undifferentiated member of some group. In such cases, the normal psychological process of categorization has negative outcomes.

Stereotypes Can be Isolating

Jane Chen and Cheryl Ho, both from Honolulu, found themselves interacting frequently at a convention of Asian American businesspeople in San Francisco. Jane and Cheryl had attended different high schools and had never met each other prior to the convention. They found that they recently had similar job experiences. Both had been representing their companies in small cities in Midwestern states: Jane in Nebraska and Cheryl in Minnesota. There were very few other Chinese Americans in the two cities.

They discovered that their experiences were similar. They were asked about how it feels to be a member of a model minority group. People wanted to fix them up with eligible Chinese American males whom they knew. In their workplaces, they were treated as if they were quiet individuals without well-developed opinions. Children who had not yet learned their social skills stared at them in the grocery store. "I have felt like an exhibit at a zoo," they both thought at one time or another.

Jane and Cheryl are experiencing the results of stereotyping. Whenever there is a collection of people to whom others can apply a label, stereotypes can result. Labels can be of many kinds: Republicans, absent minded professors, feminists, and the names of various ethnic and cultural groups. A key aspect of stereotypes is that once the label is assigned, then a great deal of information from the stereotype is applied to the labeled individual. This can be very frustrating for people who do not want to be placed into the stereotype. "Not all Chinese-Americans are quiet bookworms and former high school valedictorians who use chopsticks all the time," Jane and Cheryl agreed. Some Chinese Americans are good banjo players who may enjoy hearing about the informal gatherings organized by musicians interested in country-western music. But if others place Chinese Americans into the traditional stereotype that has a long history, country-western music will not come to mind and so invitations to musical gatherings will not be forthcoming.

If people are given a label and treated accordingly, then "stereotype exhaustion" can be a result. In this example, the Chinese Americans become exhausted from the number of times they have to explain themselves, respond to negative expectations, and react to workplace behaviors that can put them at a disadvantage compared to their coworkers. They enjoy returning to San Francisco and Honolulu where they are not constantly the targets of stereotyped expectations.

Good advice for hosts is that they should seek out information about individuals that have absolutely no relationship to a stereotype. People might also think about stereotypes that another person might apply to them and consider how unreasonable these can be.

ATTRIBUTIONS

Once people have organized their knowledge into well-established categories, they quickly form judgments about themselves and others based on these categories (Park, Choi, & Cho, 2006; Ross, 1997). The category "edible foods" quickly leads to judgments of good food and bad food. The category "proper behaviors in the workplace" quickly leads to judgments about which people are good and poor colleagues.

Judgments about People's Behaviors: Personal and Professional Styles

Jung-Mi Kim and Yeon-Hee Pak had been classmates at a women's college in Seoul, Korea. After graduation, Jung-Mi had attended graduate school in the United States and then worked in the human resources department of a large American company. Yeon-Hee accepted employment in the accounting department of a Korean company that manufactured construction materials.

Jung-Mi Kim had developed the reputation as a good trainer in the United States, with a specialty in improving the leadership skills of young managers. She was asked to give a workshop at the company where Yeon-Hee worked. Jung-Mi gave a dynamic leadership improvement workshop. She demonstrated an energetic speaking style and confident body movements as she engaged the attention of workshop participants. Yeon-Hee thought that Jung-Mi had developed an overly direct and assertive personality and was uncomfortable talking with her former college classmate.

Yeon-Hee has risked making an attribution error (Park et al, 2006). Attributions refer to judgments about the causes of behavior. Perhaps without conscious thought, people make such judgments every day. The boss complimented our work. Is this sincere, or does he want our support as he goes up for promotion? A colleague is abrupt with us during a phone call. Is she being rude, or is she especially busy today? Our answers to questions like these are called "attributions."

In this example, Yeon-Hee may be making a very basic attribution error. She may be making conclusions about Jung-Mi's personality traits and not taking into account the context that has surrounded her in the United States. Rather than conclude that Jung-Mi is overly direct and assertive, Yeon-Hee should consider her former classmate's recent experiences. In the United States, a forceful and dynamic presentation style is valued, and Jung-Mi has learned to give workshops using this style. This does not mean the Jung-Mi's personality has changed. It means that she has learned to be effective in a different context: training workshops that meet the expectations of businesspeople in the United States. One reason for this attribution is that people are familiar with traits they like and dislike. However, they are not as familiar with the social contexts where other people have worked successfully in recent years.

To deal with the possibility of this attribution error, people must set aside judgments based on personalities and to consider carefully various aspects of social contexts that could be influencing the behavior of others (Hine, Montiel, Cooksey, & Lewko (2005).

SOCIAL CONTEXT: THE FREQUENTLY OVERLOOKED CAUSE OF BEHAVIOR

In making attributional errors, then, people focus on the traits on individuals about whom they are making judgments and overlook the situational factors that may be influencing them (Blass, 2004; Ross, 1977; Zimbardo and Lieppe, 1991). One reason is that people think of personality as highly stable. If people believe in the stability of personality, then they will observe the behaviors of others and will make conclusions that behaviors follow from stable personality traits. In actuality, as seen in the incident about Jung-Mi and the training style she uses in the United States, people adjust their behaviors to meet the demands of various social situations. Another reason for overlooking social situations is that their features are relatively invisible to outsiders. We see individuals behaving and are tempted to make attributions based on their personalities, that is, on the basis of their personal qualities. But the situational demands to which they are responding, such as work deadlines, aging parents, and financial pressures are often invisible unless people know the others extremely well. Sometimes, especially when the situations to be faced are in the future, situational pressures are invisible to both observers and to people who will be experiencing the situations.

SOCIAL CONTEXT CAN HAVE STRONG PULL ON BEHAVIOR

People who knew both Seiko Koga and Kenji Mitsui thought that they were an ideal couple. Seiko and Kenji met when both were working for Japanese-owned hotels in Hawaii. Earlier in their lives, both had been participants in exchange programs that took them to schools in the Eastern United States. In Hawaii, Seiko and Kenji dated and enjoyed their walks on the beach, drives up Tantalus to view sunsets, and moonlit dinners in outdoor restaurants. They seemed to have endless time for each other and vowed that, after marriage, their love would never change.

After a year in Hawaii, they married and returned to jobs in Tokyo. Gradually, Seiko and Kenji felt that their lives were changing. Kenji observed that the men who obtained promotions spent long hours in the office and then spent time with coworkers in various nightclubs. Because of the high cost of living, they rented a small apartment that demanded an hour's subway commute to work. Occasionally, Kenji missed the last train given the demands of after-hours carousing with clients. He would have to rent a hotel room, adding to expenses. Friends back in Hawaii were saddened to learn that Seiko and Kenji were talking about a divorce five years after their return to Japan.

Complex decisions such as whether to divorce will be influenced by cultural, economic, and personal reasons. Any discussion of culture must include the fact that Seiko and Kenji courted in one place and then spent the first years of their marriage in a quite different place. In Hawaii, they courted according to cultural norms such as spending large amounts of time together, vowing to never change their commitment, and exchanging many romantic gestures. Back in Japan, they had to adjust to a quite different set of cultural expectations that had a major impact on their marriage. In addition to the workplace demands Kenji faced, Seiko might be frustrated with her career advancement, given limited promotion possibilities for women and pressures that she quit work and have children.

While admittedly adding expense to marriage plans, dating couples like Kenji and Seiko might consider an extended visit to the city where they will eventually live. There, they would ask questions such as, "What will be the cultural expectations placed on us and what sorts of extensive effort will be necessary to have a successful marriage?"

REGULARLY OCCURRING SOCIAL SITUATION CAN LEAD TO DEFENSE MECHANISMS

The importance of understanding social situations cannot be overstated. People have the ability to think about the situational pressures they face now and may face in the future, and they can then make adjustments to their behavior. If social situations recur regularly, people often develop habitual ways of dealing with them. In the first incident in this chapter involving the two Chinese-American women, Jane and Cheryl have undoubtedly developed strategies for dealing with people who place them into a stereotyped category. They may relate personal information about themselves in an attempt to force people's thinking beyond the stereotype. Or, they may identify an element from the stereotype ("I really don't like Chinese food very much") to force others to think in more complex terms.

In this incident, an American interacts with a Czech colleague and makes an incorrect attribution because he does not understand the concept that people develop ways of dealing with regularly recurring situations.

Protecting against Possible Disappointments

"I'm glad they changed the name to the Czech Republic," Barry Miller thought as he looked out his office window to see a gray February day in Prague. "Czechoslovakia was the word I always missed during our school spelling bees back in Toledo, Ohio." Barry shared this thought with Petr Bozek, a coworker at a sporting goods company for which they both worked. Barry found that Petr was not the sort of person who made friends quickly, and so he was pleased when Petr agreed to have lunch one day.

At the lunch, the coworkers talked about upcoming events in their personal lives as well as developments in the company. Petr mentioned that he was planning to go skiing during the upcoming weekend. He added, "But the snow probably won't be very good and the ski lifts may be broken, as in the past." When they talked about new technology at work, Petr warned Barry that the company's new computers would probably be out of date by the time they were installed. Further, the electricity in their building would probably be inadequate to support sophisticated computers. Barry was struck by the gloomy tone in Petr's conversation.

Petr is engaging in behaviors called "defensive pessimism." In addition to the Czech Republic, this style of thinking and conversing with others is found in many Eastern European countries. Given the experiences of World War II, and the unwelcome influence of communism after the war, people in the Czech Republic had to accustom themselves to various privations. One way to deal with limited resources and the real possibility of disappointment is to have limited expectations. Then, if people actually experience the limitations, they are not disappointed since they expected no better. However, if they have positive experiences, they are even more welcome since they exceeded expectations.

In Petr's case, he tells Barry that he expects poor snow, broken ski lifts, and outdated computers. If reality meets these expectations, he has protected himself against disappointment. If the ski trip is successful and if the computers are "state of the art," then he is happy that his expectations were exceeded. The danger with defensive pessimism is that it can lead to inaction if people reinforce each other with their negative thinking and communications. There can be little positive action for the future unless people move forward with bold, positive, and optimistic behaviors that will improve developing economies.

While people can change their habitual behaviors, they usually must be motivated to do so. Petr might try to demonstrate a more optimistic conversational style if he learns that Barry has a negative reaction to the more pessimistic style. But change is always difficult and it demands time and energy, which Petr might devote to other aspects of his personal or professional life. Another difficulty is that even though people might consider modifying their behavior, older and well-established ways of behaving are likely to be expressed when they are under situational pressures that are stressful.

Intense Emotions Can Lead to Practiced
and Familiar Behaviors

The Human Relations specialists at Bartlett Accounting in Seattle had been planning the employee recognition dinner for two months. The company had established the goal of greater participation in international business ventures ten years ago. Hard work and patience had paid off, and the company now had offices in eight countries. At the Seattle headquarters, company executives were pleased to announce that the "employee of the year award" recipient was Kyong Hee Cho, originally from Suwon, Korea.

Kyong Hee's parents were so proud of her achievement that they traveled to Seattle for the recognition dinner. Kyong Hee was allowed to choose who would do the actual award presentation, and she selected her immediate supervisor, John McNeil. After the dinner, the presentations of awards started. The master of ceremonies called for John and Kyong Hee to come forward. John then described Kyong Hee's many accomplishments and handed her a plaque and a monetary award. Audience members started applauding loudly. The master of ceremonies said to John, "For Heaven's sake, give her a hug." John did so, but Kyong Hee was obviously uncomfortable with this aspect of the award presentation.

There are at least two issues in this incident that are worth examining. One is a cultural difference. In Korea, physical contact between males and females in public settings is far less frequent than in the United States. Especially when many people are present, as at the awards banquet, Kyong Hee is likely to become very uncomfortable.

The other issue deals with a more general aspect of human behavior. When people are excited, they don't think carefully about various ways of behaving. Rather, they behave in ways that are very familiar and that have been practiced many times. At the banquet, people were excited and were applauding. The master of ceremonies got caught up in the emotions of the moment and said something that is very familiar to him, "give her a hug." Given the excitement, he was not likely to stop and consider the cultural appropriateness of physical contact between males and females. Further, he was not likely to consider recent workplace recommendations in the United States that ask people to think carefully about the implications of traditional gestures such as a hug.

Certain factors can intensify habitual and well-established behaviors. Kyong Hee's parents are at the awards dinner, and this will increase her discomfort and will be a reminder of the Korean norms that are more familiar to her.

SELF-REFERENCING AND SOCIAL IDENTITY

As part of people's socialization into their culture, people spend a great deal of time learning appropriate categories and appropriate items for those categories (Berry, Poortinga, & Panday, 1997). In the business world, people are promoted because they can demonstrate behaviors associated with categories such as "good boss," "effective marketer," and "loyal employee." Given their successes with such categories, it is not surprising that they think of themselves in positive terms. That is, they experience positive self-esteem and feel that they have a social identity that is appreciated by others in their culture.

When these successful people interact with people in other cultures, it is natural that they begin their thinking and their choices about behavior with what they already know. There is the danger, however, of limits to people's thinking if they only work with ideas and behaviors that are already familiar. They must move beyond thinking based solely on their own feelings and reactions and must instead strive to accommodate unfamiliar information that they encounter in other cultures.

Moving Beyond Self-Referencing in Decision Making

When I took calculus in college, the professor would often assign very difficult problems and also problems that were impossible to solve. However, he would not accept a student's claim that "I can't do it, and so it can't be done!" He wanted students to specify exactly why a problem could not be solved. For example, he expected students to tell what information is missing and must be supplied if the problem is to be solved. This was my first introduction to the concept of "self-referencing."

When people base decisions solely on their own reactions, life experiences, and preferences, they are engaging in self-referencing. To make more informed decisions, they need to integrate other information: the views of others, the experiences of people who have faced similar problems in different countries, the lessons from history available from trips to the library, and the preferences of many people assessed through questionnaires and opinion polls.

Julie Lee, a marketing professor, has taught at the University of Hawaii. She is from Australia and knows that there is a very popular food product there that many Americans find inedible. Vegemite is a popular spread for crackers and bread in Australia, but to many Americans it tastes like fermented yeast paste. Dr. Lee asks American students to taste vegemite, and then asks them to design a marketing plan. Her goal is to move students beyond the self-referencing criterion, "I don't like it and so there is no market for it."

Another way of communicating the importance of understanding self-referencing is to blindfold people and ask them to distinguish fine California from French wines, or to distinguish Coke from Pepsi. People are given sips of the wines or soft drinks and are asked to tell which is which. Many people, if they have experience with fine wines or the soft drinks, think they can make the distinctions. While blindfolded, most people cannot tell the difference between the wines or between the soft drinks. This experience hopefully encourages people to move beyond the self-referenced statement, "I think I can do it and so it will be easy to do."

One of the benefits of extensive interactions with people from other cultures is that people must move beyond self-referencing to have good interpersonal relationships. People in different cultures grow up eating different foods, enjoying diverse leisure time activities, developing friendships in different ways, and participating in diverse educational systems. When they interact with people from other cultures, they learn that they cannot talk solely about their own experiences and engage only in their preferred activities. They must move beyond self-referencing to take other people's preferences into account.

Once people become sensitive to the points of view of people from other cultures, they often find that their personal worldviews expand. They become more open-minded people with more complex personal identities. People's identities are not static. They constantly develop as people accept various life roles such as marriage partner, parent, teacher, boss, church elder, and community volunteer. Experiences with individuals from other cultures become another opportunity to expand a person's identity. The complexity of people's social identities can be seen in this incident.

People's Identities Adjust to Meet Their Everyday Goals

"What a coincidence to meet in Sweden," Jane Chun said to Ron Kealoha after meeting by chance on a street in Stockholm. Jane and Ron worked for different branches of the same large bank in Honolulu and would see each other two or three times a year. With their spouses, they vacationed in Europe and became enthusiastic about sharing reactions with others from their same hometown. The four tourists had dinner together and shared a day of sightseeing. Jane and Ron promised to contact each other when they returned to Honolulu, but they never did. Even though each considered contacting the other, this intention did not lead to telephone calls.

One explanation for the enthusiastic interactions in Stockholm coupled with no contact back in Honolulu is that people have very flexible identities. Identities refer to people's views about themselves, and they can be measured by asking people to complete a series of self-statements all beginning with, "I am..." People often make the mistake of thinking that identities are very consistent and stable from year to year. In reality, people have very loose collections of self-statements that summarize flexible social identities. This flexibility is very useful as people work toward the accomplishment of various goals in various social situations.

In Stockholm, Jane and Ron would have the self-statements, "I am a tourist." With this aspect of their identities in the forefront, they would enjoy interacting with someone from their hometown. In another country, it is comfortable to use familiar language and to share reactions based on similar cultural experiences in their own lives. Back in Honolulu, self-statements about being a tourist fade into the background. Other aspects of their identities take center stage, such as "I am in charge of a project at the bank." If Jane and Ron are not working on similar projects, there may be little reason for them to schedule a meeting or to have lunch together.

This incident and analysis developed from conversations with Karen Lee, office of the president at the University of Hawaii. Because of her father's career in international technical assistance, she grew up in New Zealand, Cameroon, and the Philippines. People who know two or more cultures may be especially sensitive to the fact that social identities are flexible. One year, Karen would say, "I am a student in Cameroon," and the next year there would be a change given that she had become a student in the Philippines. There would be different goals, such as making friends and adjusting to new school curricula, to which she would attach various aspects of her flexible social identity.

Clearly, I am recommending that sojourners become flexible and learn to pick up cues concerning how their behavioral options should expand when they interact with people from other cultures. Such expansion can affect how people eventually think about themselves since they will realize that they have become more flexible in response to cultural cues. The expansion of self-identity will also lead to greater workplace effectiveness since people can adjust their managerial and collegial styles to take into account host preferences.

Work in Groups Can Affect Individual Contributions

As a project manager for a software engineering firm in Cupertino, California, Mary Riley was accustomed to working with highly independent computer specialists. Her coworkers were very creative, liked to work on projects of their own choosing, and preferred working alone rather than in groups. Mary once tried to introduce team-based projects, but results were disappointing. When they worked in teams, people had a difficult time sharing their ideas for fear that others would not give them proper credit for their original thinking. If they developed a product that could be patented or copyrighted, the computer specialists feared that they would not earn as much money as they felt they deserved.

A year ago, Mary accepted a management position in Bangkok, Thailand. Noting her past experience, her supervisors asked her to oversee projects that involved innovative computer technology for rural development work. She was told that any new products and programs could have uses in other Asian countries. In sharp contrast to her experiences in California, Mary found that the Thai computer specialists enjoyed working as part of teams. They were highly productive, helped each other when stumbling blocks occurred, and were willing to share credit for various innovations. Mary wondered why group efforts were effective in one culture but not the other.

Mary is encountering an aspect of people's social identity. In the United States, many people have an "independent self-construal." This means that they view themselves as individual actors who are judged on the basis of their unique contributions.

Throughout their formal education, they worked on various projects for which they would be held responsible: term papers, class presentations, science fair projects, and so forth. They become very good at identifying projects on which they want to work, and they are willing to be judged as successful or unsuccessful when they complete their efforts. If they do join groups, they may engage in "social loafing." Since it is hard for outsiders to judge their individual contributions to a group, they may work with less intensity. Group efforts become less than the sum of potential individual contributions.

In Thailand and other Asian countries, many people have an "interdependent self-construal." This means that they view themselves as members of groups, and these groups can consist of family members, school friends, coworkers, and others with whom they are in frequent contact. As part of their formal schooling, teachers expected them to contribute to class projects and to form study groups with schoolmates. When they become part of teams, they often experience "social striving." Being part of a group energizes them and allows them to express their interdependent identity and to benefit from the contributions of others.

Change is imminent. Realizing that technology-based projects demand the contributions of many specialists, American executives have asked business school faculty to introduce team building skills so that graduates are better prepared to work effectively in groups.

14

Some Final Pieces of Advice and Some Concluding Perspectives

A great deal of ground has been covered. A wide range of issues surrounding intercultural experiences have been discussed. These include the process of adjusting to other cultures, dealing with cultural differences such as individualism and collectivism (Brewer & Chen, 2007; Triandis, 1995), interpreting different communication styles, making decisions, dealing with gender differences, understanding workplace dynamics, and developing close interpersonal relationships. While all these issues in intercultural interactions can lead to problems that can affect adjustment and communication, the chances of effectiveness (Shay & Baack, 2004) can be increased if people are well prepared. People need to avoid the thought that "I am the only one who is having problems adjusting to other cultures!" They need to substitute this thought with another, "Everyone has problems, but I can meet the challenges inherent in intercultural communication."

CULTURAL INFORMANTS

While this book has contained many discussions of cultural differences people are likely to encounter, it cannot possibly cover all potential difficulties. My goal has been to present a large number of potential stumbling blocks to sensitize and to prepare readers for intercultural challenges. But they will face other challenges in their actual interactions. In this final chapter, I'd like to present a few pieces of advice that will help them go beyond the specific examples in this book. In addition, I'd like to discuss some benefits that people are likely to find if they develop close intercultural relationships.

One excellent strategy for dealing with potential cultural misunderstandings is to nurture relationships with hosts who can discuss problems and who can suggest possible interventions.

Relations with Cultural Informants Can Assist Adjustment

Just before leaving for his three-year assignment in Norway, Ross Devereux stopped by the Human Resources office of the engineering firm where he worked in Boulder, Colorado. He wanted to speak with Sharon Tyler, who had organized a training program to assist in his adjustment to Norway. "I'm sure you'll do well as a sojourner to another country," Sharon told Ross. "Be sure to develop relations with people who might become cultural informants. Returnees from overseas tell me that this is especially important." Ross admitted, "With all the material covered during training, I don't remember everything about cultural informants. Could you remind me?"

Cultural informants are host national individuals who are good at answering questions that will assist people from other countries who are going through the adjustment process (Brislin & Yoshida, 1994; Rubenfeld, Clement, Vinograd, Lussier, Auger, & Lebrun, 2007). In Ross's case, this would mean a Norwegian who is willing to answer his questions about cultural differences, challenges to a smooth adjustment, and standard work practices in Norway. In addition to their willingness to talk regularly with newcomers from other countries, cultural informants have other qualities. They have worked with enough sojourners to have seen what causes them to have the most adjustment difficulties. Often, the informants have themselves lived in another country and so have had typical sojourner experiences: being puzzled by cultural differences, loneliness and homesickness, difficulties communicating effectively with host nationals, and so forth.

Cultural informants often enjoy developing relationships with sojourners. Most sojourners eventually make a successful adjustment and develop feelings of self-confidence that they can deal with any difficulties that life brings to them. By interacting with sojourners, cultural informants can be reminded of their own adjustment successes and can also share interests based on their international experiences. Often, interacting with sojourners becomes the only opportunity for informants to use their hard-won, highly valued international knowledge.

In his discussion with Sharon, Ross brought up a point about training programs that will always be troublesome. So much information is presented that not all of it can possibly find a place in a person's memory. Cultural informants can provide frequent reminders of cultural practices that may have been covered during training but that were imperfectly remembered. In Hawaii, informants would remind newcomers, "Always take your shoes off before entering someone's house." In many Asian countries, good advice is, "Be very careful about disagreeing with others in public." People do not distinguish the perceived worth of their ideas from the perceived worth of themselves as human beings. In Germany, the advice might be, "No matter what topic you might bring up during informal conversations, be prepared for someone to turn it into a serious discussion that will remind you of your most difficult college courses." If people can avoid the social embarrassment of making culturally based social errors, their adjustment will be smoother.

Many times, especially in formal encounters with hosts, sojourners will deal with professional interpreters (Mindess, 1999). These professionals can be especially helpful, and it is wise to work with them in ways that allow them to carry out their jobs most effectively (Noe, Hollenbeck, Gerhart, & Wright, 2008).

Working with Interpreters at International Conferences

"I attended an international conference on global markets," a businessman recently told me, "and presentations were translated into a number of languages. Listening on earphones, some of the talks were very clear and others were not. I will be speaking at a similar international conference in the future. Do you have any advice for me?"

First, some definitions (Brislin, MacNab, & Bechtold, 2004). When moving from one language to another, "translation" is the term used for written documents. When language use is oral, the term "interpretation" is used. In simultaneous interpretation, a speaker begins and interpreters immediately follow in another language. Often, interpreters take advantage of a speaker's natural pauses, but the speaker does not schedule long stops during the presentation. This is a very difficult task and it is part of a four- or five-year college curriculum in interpreter training. In consecutive interpretation, a speaker covers a section of the material and then stops. The interpreters present this material in the other language, and then the speaker begins again with another section of the presentation.

To increase the chances of success at international conferences, my advice is to work closely with interpreters. Far too often, speakers show up at their appointed time and sometimes do not even meet their interpreters. Speakers begin, and interpreters follow from their booths filled with electronic equipment. A far better procedure is to meet with interpreters prior to the scheduled talk. Speakers can give the interpreters a copy of the presentation. They can ask whether their new colleagues prefer simultaneous or consecutive interpretation. Speakers can emphasize major points and can suggest what they would like audience members to remember six months after the conference. Speakers can go over difficult terms and can give specific examples of complex concepts.

Speakers must keep in mind that interpreters cannot possibly have advanced knowledge in all fields. If the talk deals with financial markets, interpreters may be very well-educated but may not have attended a business school. Speakers must have enough common sense to identify difficult concepts and, at times, to change their presentations based on feedback from the interpreters. Often, interpreters must be given time to develop equivalent terms in another language. "Confucian cultural dynamism" is a recent term in business research that refers to aspects of Chinese philosophy that can affect economic expansion in fast-moving marketplaces. Unless they have seen a copy of the presentation, interpreters might have to come up with an equivalent term at the moment they are interpreting for the speaker. They may come up with a good equivalent, but chances of a clumsy and misleading term are high. Speakers can help their interpreters, and at the same time help themselves, by reviewing such terms and by benefiting from the interpreters' previous experiences at international conferences.

Interpreters can often act as cultural informants, giving advice that goes beyond the language that they choose to use. They can often answer questions such as, "What is a good way to start my presentation to this audience? Is it likely that the audience members will want to ask questions? What is a typical amount of time given to questions and answers for a one hour talk? Is there anything I should know about appropriate behaviors that I should engage in after the talk?" The more specific the questions, the more the interpreter will be able to help.

BENEFITING FROM EXTENSIVE INTERCULTURAL INTERACTIONS

While the challenges of developing and maintaining intercultural interactions are many, the benefits to be derived from successful relationships with culturally different others are considerable (Kagitcibasi, 1978). For example, intercultural interactions can encourage people to move beyond the ethnocentric set of beliefs that the way people behave in their own culture should be the standard for the world. If people have successful intercultural interactions, they inevitably learn that people in different cultures can behave in a variety of ways to obtain their goals. Further, behavior makes sense only if people's socialization into a culture and their goal setting are understood. In addition to challenges to ethnocentrism, intercultural experiences also force people to think through their prejudices.

I will be discussing both ethnocentrism and prejudice, and I should make distinctions between the two since the terms are often used interchangeably. Ethnocentrism refers to the careless and unthinking imposition of the standards for daily life and proper behavior that people learned as part of socialization into their own culture. For example, people learn to meet and to greet newcomers into their lives (Chapter 12). Appropriate behaviors can include enthusiasm, a handshake, and the statement that "it is nice to meet you." People are being ethnocentric if they think that individuals from other cultures should meet and greet in the same manner. Often, ethnocentric judgments include the conclusions that people from other cultures are ignorant, socially inept, or backwards in their thinking.

At times, ethnocentric thinking is so subtle that even well-meaning people who want to be sensitive to cultural differences make mistakes during their intercultural interactions.

Attempting to Be Socially Skilled

As part of a five-year plan that she developed with her workplace mentors in Atlanta, Georgia, Susan Phillips accepted a two-year assignment in the Philippines. Shortly after her arrival in Manila, she found that she had been invited to a reception at the home of the company president. She talked to several of her new coworkers about what would be an appropriate dress to wear. One, Patricia Santos, offered to take Susan to a nice dress shop.

Patricia offered to drive and picked up Susan early one morning. They drove about ten miles through stop-and-go traffic to reach a dress shop. Patricia said, "It is a good idea to arrive at a store early. Shop owners often give a discount to the first customer each day to bring them good luck for the rest of the day." Susan did her shopping and made a purchase.

Patricia and Susan then decided to drive to their workplace. Patricia had to stop at a gas station, and Susan offered to help pay for the gas. "You must have used quite a bit of gas during the trip since we had to stop so often," Susan said. Patricia insisted she could pay and was very quiet after leaving the gas station.

Susan is trying to be socially skilled. In her country, people often offer to pitch in and pay for gas when an errand is being run for their benefit. In the Philippines, Patricia feels insulted that her hospitality is being questioned and that money is being offered after she demonstrated her friendliness and willingness to help. Nobody is trying to be culturally insensitive, but Susan can be considered guilty of ethnocentrism for believing that her views about social skills are applicable in Manila.

Many times, people move beyond the cognitions surrounding ethnocentrism into the emotional realm of prejudice. They conclude that the behaviors of people in other cultures are not only different, they are wrong, backward, and unreasonable! When people engage in prejudicial behaviors, they put members of other groups at a disadvantage. Because of their group membership, these others are denied opportunities such as advanced education and training, invitations to social events where networks might be developed, and informal communication channels where work-related information is shared. The placement into "other groups" can be based on any reason that creates real and perceived differences among people. These reasons include race, ethnicity, gender, physical handicaps, age, social class background, political affiliation, and religion.

Some prejudices are based on people's cherished values learned during socialization into their culture. These people become irritated with members of other groups who do not seem to share these values. This form of prejudice is called "symbolic racism." The term comes from analyses of culture that show that all people have very important symbols. These symbols can be objects, such as texts, flags, and cherished artifacts. Or, the symbols can be learned concepts such as "individuals should be judged by the amount of hard work that they do," or "when individuals have difficulties, they should pick themselves up by their bootstraps." If people have prejudices based on symbolism and values, they claim that they have nothing against other groups. The people continue, "It is just that these others do not behave in appropriate ways. If they just changed their behavior, everything would be okay."

The best way to understand prejudices based on values and symbolism is to begin with deep-seated feelings that are held by people. Then, their attitudes toward other groups can be examined with these feelings in mind. For example, many people believe that success in work and life is based on a strong work ethic. Much of their personal identity as worthwhile individuals is based on their jobs and careers. If these people think that members of other groups do not share this value about the importance of hard work, then they will not treat the others with respect. It is important to remember that there are many reasons why people are placed in groups. If men feel that they have to be tough when important business decisions are made, they may deny women opportunities to rise into managerial and executive ranks. The men continue, "You sometimes have to make enemies when it comes to tough decisions. Women are too soft."

Prejudices based on symbols and values can sometimes be changed through extensive interactions with people from other cultural groups. Recognizing this benefit, and other outcomes such as expanded worldviews, I have long worked with administrators of programs that offer overseas study and travel. If people live in another culture, they will inevitably see differences in everyday behaviors meant to solve basic life problems. Through intercultural experiences, people often develop the self-insight that they were socialized to have one set of values. But it is not the only set of values that people use to satisfy the goals they set for themselves. "One size does not have to fit all!" when considering cultures and people's values.

THE BENEFITS OF INTERCULTURAL EXPERIENCE

If people accept the challenges of intercultural experiences and move beyond ethnocentrism, there are other benefits that may await them (Fisher, Maes, & Schmitt, 2007; Fu & Chiu, 2007; Kagitcibasi, 1978; Milstein, 2005). These include increased self-confidence and an increased interest in world events. It should be emphasized, however, that these benefits might not occur immediately. Sojourners may face reverse culture shock (Bolino, 2007; Steyn & Grant, 2007) after their return to their own country (Chapter 2), and this can cause stress in their personal and professional lives. The benefits of intercultural experiences become clear after sojourners readjust to their own country.

Overseas Assignments Can Lead to Personal Change

After a two-year assignment in Germany, Michelle Parton was greeted enthusiastically by her coworkers in her company's home office in Chicago. Always a well-liked boss and colleague, Michelle had kept in touch with people in Chicago during her overseas assignment. For her first year back in the United States, Michelle had worked in her company's office in Boston and completed arrangements for a joint business venture with a German Organization. She then returned to the home office in Chicago where she had worked for five years prior to the assignment in Germany. After a few weeks during which colleagues observed her at meetings, lunches, and company-sponsored social events, many commented that "Michelle seems to have changed." This was not a negative feeling, but rather a comment on her work, her interaction style, and the topics she brought up during conversations. However, Michelle's colleagues could not be precise when describing the changes that they observed.

Michelle and her colleagues are dealing with the changes that often occur as a result of overseas assignments. The people who undertook the assignments, called sojourners, know that they think and feel differently about many aspects of their lives, and their friends and colleagues sense these changes. However, people have a difficult time describing the changes that they either have experienced or have observed. One change is that returnees from overseas assignments often have an increased sense of self-confidence and sense of personal achievement. They inevitably faced challenges during their assignments, and so they were forced to meet them and to overcome difficulties. In addition, the sojourners were far away from their home offices and so had to solve problems using their own initiative and creativity. Returnees often develop a "can do" attitude that they bring back to their companies.

Returnees develop a broader perspective on current events and develop a greater sense of worldmindedness. They see firsthand how developments in one part of the world affect policies in other parts. They inevitably find themselves in discussions where people express very different opinions and introduce arguments with which they are unfamiliar. These experiences lead sojourners to see issues and problems from the point of view of people in other countries. This leads to an expansion of their thinking and the possibility of innovative and creative contributions to discussions back in their companies' home offices.

This interest in world events extends beyond specific issues in any one country. Michelle is likely to become more sophisticated in her thinking about events in many countries. This will be especially true in her case since world politics and international events are favorite topics of conversation when Germans socialize. Michelle is also likely to become interested in other issues related to overseas assignments such as adjustment to other cultures, overcoming difficulties, and the content of training programs meant to ease the stresses brought on by movement across cultural boundaries.

Sojourners often develop greater insights into the contributions of coworkers and how different people bring different talents to workplace tasks. In their own countries, people who have been on the job for several years learn to deal with the same coworkers. It becomes easy for people to take each other for granted. On overseas assignments, people have to meet and interact with a new group of coworkers. They have to figure out what people's skills are and how to use these skills to achieve company goals. They have to think carefully about their coworkers and cannot rely on facile assumptions based on superficial characteristics. They can call upon this same careful thinking during work assignments after their return.

Returnees often find that their job descriptions expand. In their home offices, they are asked to contribute to tasks that have an international component. In Michelle's case, she would likely be included in company meetings that involved visitors from Germany. After these meetings, she would likely be asked for her perspective and predictions for the future, given her previous assignment in Germany.

MUTUALLY ACCEPTABLE AGREEMENTS DURING NEGOTIATIONS

Michelle's superiors will be wise to include her when dealing with German businesspeople who may want to propose an international joint venture. Knowing about cultural differences can be of great assistance in negotiations with counterparts from other countries. This type of knowledge can assist in the development of policies that benefit all parties involved and that will stimulate all parties to invest resources into the successful application of the policies. Intercultural negotiations are never simple, but steps can be taken to increase the chances of success.

Biases in People's Thinking Can Derail Negotiations

Having set a goal that labor costs must be reduced, the company for which Lester Martin served as a vice president considered importing goods from China rather than manufacturing them in the United States. Lester's company manufactured and marketed specialized protective clothing products for industries such as home pest extermination, asbestos removal, and laboratory work for technicians who worked with potentially dangerous microorganisms. Traveling to Shanghai, Lester met with executives of various Chinese organizations in the hopes of obtaining an agreement for a joint venture. He felt that he had a good business plan that would be attractive to his Chinese counterparts. He pointed out the number of jobs that would be created in Shanghai and the high quality of the housing development he proposed for Chinese workers. Lester was disappointed that the Chinese executives did not share his vision.

Carsten De Dreu (2005) has identified biases in people's thinking that are especially troublesome during negotiations. Lester may have succumbed to both. One bias is called ego defensiveness. People want to maintain a positive self-view of themselves. They want to view themselves as reasonable individuals who think carefully about problems and who make good decisions. In Lester's case, this positive self-evaluation would include the ability to develop a good business plan that would bring benefits both to his company and to any Chinese company that enters into a joint venture. Given that Lester has had success in his own country, rising to the level of a company vice president, he will be especially anxious to protect his positive self-image.

One way to protect this image is to view others who seem uninterested in his proposal as unreasonable, overly competitive, and incompetent to make good decisions. If Lester feels this way, he is likely to communicate his negative feelings in the course of negotiations with his Chinese counterparts. Since the counterparts also have healthy egos and positive self-evaluations, they may reciprocate the negative feelings. After several rounds of such communications between Lester and his counterparts, the negotiations are likely to spiral into intense negativity. Eventually, they may break down before any agreements are reached.

Another bias in thinking is called naïve realism. Negotiations about complex matters are always difficult and stressful. One way that people attempt to cut through the complexity is to simplify the issues under discussion. They can do this by developing a view of reality that is based on the assumption that everyone thinks like they do. Further, they feel that if others don't share their views, then these others are ignorant and unmotivated to contribute to positive changes. Of course, this is naïve: Different people think in a wide variety of ways and have diverse opinions. In Lester's case, he is assuming that his views of what his company can offer China are exactly what the Chinese counterparts want. Lester points to the number of jobs that will be created and the quality of his proposed housing development. The Chinese may be interested in other aspects of a possible joint venture. They may be interested in the amount of job security workers will have and the site of the manufacturing plant. The Chinese may be interested in a plant that will be built in a rural area if they feel that Shanghai is overcrowded and that too many people have moved to the city from small villages.

Steps can be taken to minimize the negative effects of ego defensiveness and naïve realism. De Dreu (2005) suggests that negotiators give attention to four factors. The first is the relative amount of power possessed by the different parties in the negotiation. The second is increasing the accountability of the negotiation process. The third is developing a cooperative rather then competitive orientation during the negotiations. The fourth factor is using time to the advantage of the negotiation process.

These steps work well when negotiators desire an agreement that meets the interest of all parties involved. The goal of negotiations is not to grind opponents into the dirt or to treat them "as flies to wanton boys" (King Lear). The problem with such negotiations is that there will be a party that will label itself the winner, but the loser will not put time and energy into following through on agreements that the winner imposed. Instead, the members of the party not treated well will drag their feet, will challenge the agreements, and in general will work to undermine the efforts of the so-called winner. In intercultural negotiations, it is unlikely that the party whose members feel ill-treated will engage in future business ventures with the party whose members chose to be winners rather than collaborators.

If all four factors are given attention during negotiations, people move from being pro-self to pro-social thinkers. That is, they integrate their own interests with those of their counterparts. Further, they engage in careful thinking that has the goal of developing proposals that allow everyone to make progress toward goal achievement. If there is a power balance, one party cannot simply force the other to comply. If people try this, the other party has power of its own and can engage in activities such as resistance, calling in the media and giving reporters interesting stories, or public protest. If there is cooperative motivation, one party does not have the goal of bragging about being the winner. Rather, the goal is proposals that both sides can point to as benefiting all parties and as giving attention to everyone's interests.

In accountability of process, negotiators have the responsibility of explaining what happened during discussions with counterparts. The people to whom they must explain the process are their constituents. If people know they will be accountable, they are motivated to examine issues under discussion from multiple perspectives. They know they will have to stand up in front of their constituents and answer sharp questions such as, "Is the other party fully committed to following through on its concessions related to the money issues?" Finally, time can be employed to the advantage of the negotiating parties. Mild rather than intense time pressures have advantages. If deadlines for a decision allow little time for negotiations, then there will not be opportunities to do the hard work of addressing the many concerns of the different parties. But if no deadlines are set, discussions can continue to meander without any pressure to move people toward decisions about negotiated proposals of benefit to all.

References

Abelson, R. (1981). Psychological status of the script concept. *American Psychologist*, 36, 715–729.

Adler, N. (2002). *International dimensions of organizational behavior* (4th ed.). Boston, MA: PWS-Kent.

Allport, G. (1954). *The nature of prejudice*. Reading, MA: Addison-Wesley.

Aronson, E., Wilson, T., & Akert, R. (1999). *Social psychology: The heart and the mind* (4th ed.). New York: Addison-Wesley.

Bell, N. (2007). How native and non-native English speakers adapt to humor in intercultural interaction. *International Journal of Humor Research, 20*, 27–48.

Berry, J., Poortinga, Y., & Pandey, J. (1997). *Handbook of cross-cultural psychology, vol. 1: Theory and method*. Boston, MA: Allyn & Bacon.

Bhaskar-Shrinivas, P., Harrison D., Shaffer, M., & Luk, D. (2005). Input-based and time-based models of internatational adjustment: Meta-analytic evidence and theoretical extensions. *Academy of Mangement Journal, 48*, 257–281.

Bhawuk, D. P. S. (2001). Evolution of culture assimilators: Toward theory-based assimilators. *International Journal of Intercultural Relations, 25*, 141–163.

Black, J., Gregsen, H., & Mendenhall, M. (1992). *Global assignments*. San Francisco, CA: Jossey-Bass.

Blass, T. (2004). *The man who shocked the world: The life and legacy of Stanley Milgram*. New York: Basic Books.

Bochner, S. (1994). Culture shock. In W. Lonner & R. Malpass (Eds.), *Psychology and culture* (pp. 245–251). Needham Heights, MA: Allyn and Bacon.

Bochner, S. (2006). Sojourners. In D. Sam & J. Berry (Eds.), *The Cambridge handbook of acculturation psychology* (pp. 181–197). New York: Cambridge University Press.

Bolino, M. (2007). Expatriate assignments and intra-organizational career success: Implications for individuals and organizations. *Journal of International Business Studies, 38,* 819–835.

Brewer, M. (2007). The importance of being "We": Human nature and intergroup relations. *American Psychologist, 62,* 728–738.

Brewer, M., & Chen, Y. (2007). Where (who) are collectives in collectivism: Toward a conceptual clarification of individualism and collectivism. *Psychological Review, 114,* 133–151.

Brislin, R. (2000). *Understanding culture's influence on behavior* (2nd ed.). Fort Worth, TX: Harcourt.

Brislin, R., MacNab, B., & Bechtold, D. (2004). Translation between languages. In C. Spielberger (Ed.), *Encyclopedia of applied psychology* (vol. 3, pp. 587–596). Amsterdam, Netherlands and Oxford, England: Elsevier.

Brislin, R., & Yoshida, T. (1994). *Intercultural communication training: An introduction.* Thousand Oaks, CA: Sage.

Buss, D. (2000). *The dangerous passion.* New York: Free Press.

Chatard, A., Guimond, S., & Selimbegovic, L. (2007). "How good are you at math?" The effect of gender stereotypes on students' recollections of their school marks. *Journal of Experimental Social Psychology, 43,* 1017–1024.

Chen, X., Wasti, S., & Triandis, H. (2007). When does group norm or group identity predict cooperation in a public goods dilemma? The moderating effects of idiocentrism and allocentrism. *International Journal of Intercultural Relations, 31,* 259–276.

Chu, P., Spires, E., Farn, C., & Sueyoshi, T. (2005). Decision processes and use of decision aids: Comparing two closely related nations in East Asia. *Journal of Cross-Cultural Psychology, 36,* 304–320.

Cingoz, Ulu, B., & Lalonde, R. (2007). The role of culture and relational context in interpersonal conflict: Do Turks and Canadians use different conflict management strategies? *International Journal of Intercultural Relations, 31,* 443–458.

Crick, B. (1982). *In defence of politics* (2nd ed.) Middlesex, England and New York: Penguin.

Cross, S., & Gore, J. (2003). Cultural models of the self. In M. Leary & J. Tangney (Eds.), *Handbook of self and identity* (pp. 536–564). New York: Guilford.

Cushner, K., & Brislin, R. (1996). *Intercultural interactions: A practical guide* (2nd ed.). Thousand Oaks, CA: Sage.

De Dreu, C. (2005). A PACT against conflict escalation in negotiation and dispute resolution. *Current Directions in Psychological Science, 14,* 149–152.

Diener, E. (2000). Subjective well-being: The science of happiness and a proposal for a national index. *American Psychologist, 55,* 34–43.

Dinsbach, A., Feij, J., & de Vries, R. (2007). The role of communication content in an ethnically diverse organization. *International Journal of Intercultural Relations, 31,* 725–745.

Dixon, J., Durrheim, K., & Tredoux, C. (2005). Beyond the optimal contact strategy: A reality check for the contact hypothesis. *American Psychologist, 60,* 697–711.

Dunning, D., Heath, C., & Suls, J. (2004). Flawed self-assessment: Implications for health, education, and the workplace. *Psychological Science in the Public Interest* (a supplement to *Psychological Science*), *5*(3), 69–106.

Duronto, P., Nishida, T., & Nakayama, S. (2005). Uncertainty, anxiety, and avoidance in communication with strangers. *International Journal of Intercultural Relation, 29*, 549–560.

Feather, N. T. (2003). Values and deservingness in the context of organizations. In S. W. Gilliland, D. K. Steiner, & D. P. Skarliki (Eds.), *Emerging perspectives on values in organizations.* Greenwich, CT: Information Age Publishing.

Fisher, R., Maes, J., & Schmitt, M. (2007). Tearing down the "wall in the head"? Culture contact between Germans. *International Journal of Intercultural Relations, 31*, 163–179.

Foa, U., & Chemers, M. (1967). The significance of role behavior differentiation for cross-cultural interaction training. *International Journal of Psychology, 2*, 45–57.

Francesco, A., & Gold, B. (1998). *International organizational behavior.* Upper Saddle River, NJ: Prentice-Hall.

———. (2005). *International organizational behavior* (2nd ed.). Upper Saddle River, NJ: Prentice-Hall.

Fredrickson, B., & Losada, M. (2005). Positive affect and the complex dynamics of human functioning. *American Psychologist, 60*, 678–686.

Fu, J., & Chiu, C. (2007). Local culture's responses to globalization: Exemplary persons and their attendant values. *Journal of Cross-Cultural Psychology, 38*, 636–653.

Gaw, K. (2007). Mobility, multiculturalism, and marginality: Counseling third culture students. In J. Lippincott & R. Lippincott (Eds.), *Special populations in college counseling: A handbook for mental health professionals* (pp. 63–76). Alexandria, VA: American Counseling Association.

Gibson, D., & Zhong, M. (2007). Intercultural communication competence in the healthcare context. *International Journal of Intercultural Relation, 29*, 621–634.

Gilbert, G. (1998). Ordinary personology. In D. Gilbert, S. Fiske, & G. Lindzey (Eds.), *The handbook of social psychology* (vol. 2, 4th ed., pp. 89–150). New York: McGraw-Hill.

Glazer, S. (2006). Social support across cultures. *International Journal of Intercultural Relation, 30*, 605–622.

Gudykunst, W. (1998). Individualistic and collectivistic perspectives on communication: An introduction. *International Journal of Intercultural Relations, 22*, 107–134.

Gupta, A., & Govindarajan, V. (2000). Knowledge flows within MNCs. *Strategic Management Journal, 21*, 473–496.

Hall, E. (1959). *The silent language.* New York: Fawcett.

———. (1966). *The hidden dimension.* Garden City, NY: Doubleday.

Hamilton, D., & Hewstone, M. (2007). Conceptualizing group perception: A 35 year evolution. In M. Hewstone, H. Schut, J. De Wit, K. Van Den Bos, & M. Stroebe (Eds.), *The scope of social psychology: Theory and applications* (pp. 87–106). New York: Psychology Press.

Hammer, M. (1997). Negotiating across the cultural divide: Intercultural dynamics in crisis incidents. In R. Rogan, M. Hammer, & C. Van Zandt (Eds.), *Dynamic processes of crisis negotiation* (pp. 9–24). Westport, CT: Praeger.

Haugh, M. (2007). Emic conceptualizations of (im)politeness and face in Japanese: Implications for discursive negotiation of second language learner identities. *Journal of Pragmatics, 39*, 657–680.

Herskovits, M. (1948). *Man and his works*. New York: Knoph.

Hine, D., Montiel, C., Cooksey, R., & Lewko, J. (2005). Mental models of poverty in developing nations: A causal modeling analysis using a Canada-Philippines contrast. *Journal of Cross-Cultural Psychology, 36*, 283–303.

Hofstede, G. (2001). *Culture's consequences: Comparing values, behaviors, institutions, and organizations across nations* (2nd ed.). Thousand Oaks, CA: Sage.

House, R., Hanges, P., Javidan, M., Dorfman, P., & Gupta, V. (Eds.) (2004). *Culture, leadership, and organizations: The Globe Society of 62 Societies*. Thousand Oaks, CA.: Sage.

Hung, K., Li, S., & Belk, R. (2007). Glocal understandings: Female readers' perceptions of the new woman in Chinese advertising. *Journal of International Business Studies, 38*, 1034–1051.

Hyde, J. (2007). New directions in the study of gender similarities and differences. *Current Directions in Psychological Science, 16*, 259–263.

Jackson, T., Chen, H., Guo, C., & Gao, X. (2006). Stories we love by: Conceptions of love among couples from the People's Republic of China and the United States. *Journal of Cross-Cultural Psychology, 37*, 446–464.

Jandt, F. (1998). *Intercultural communication* (2nd ed.). Thousand Oaks, CA: Sage.

Janis, I. (1982). *Groupthink* (2nd ed.). Boston, MA: Houghton-Mifflin.

Kagitcibasi, C. (1978). Cross-national encounters: Turkish students in the United States. *International Journal of Intercultural Relations, 2*, 141–160.

Kaushal, R., & Kwantes, C. (2006). The role of culture and personality in choice of conflict management strategy. *International Journal of Intercultural Relation, 30*, 579–603.

Kealey, D. (1989). A study of cross-cultural effectiveness: Theoretical issues, practical applications. *International Journal of Intercultural Relations, 13*, 387–428.

———. (1996). The challenge of international personnel selection. In D. Landis & R. Bhagat (Eds.), *Handbook of intercultural training* (2nd ed.) (pp. 106–123). Thousand Oaks, CA: Sage.

Kelley, L., & Luo, Y. (1999). *China 2000: Emerging business issues*. Thousand Oaks, CA: Sage.

Klyukanov, I. (2005). *Principles of intercultural communication*. Boston, MA: Allyn & Bacon.

Leung, F. (2007). Cultural accommodation as method and metaphor. *American Psychologist, 62*, 916–927.

Levine, R. (1997). *A geography of time*. New York: Basic Books.

Littrell, R. (2007). Influences on employee preferences for empowerment practices by "the ideal" manager in China. *International Journal of Intercultural Relations, 31*, 87–110.

Lonner, W., & Malpass, R. (1994). *Psychology and culture*. Boston, MA: Allyn and Bacon.

Luo, Y., & Chen, M. (1996). Managerial implications of guanxi-based business strategies. *Journal of International Management, 2*, 293–316.

Mak, A., & Buckingham, K. (2007). Beyond communication courses: Are there benefits in adding skills-based EXCEL sociocultural training? *International Journal of Intercultural Relation, 31*, 277–291.

Mandisodza, A., Jost, J., & Unsueta, M. (2006). "Tall poppies" and "American dreams": Reactions to rich and poor in Australia and the United States. *Journal of Cross-Cultural Psychology, 37,* 659–668.

Markus, H., & Kitayama, S. (1991). Culture and the self: Implications for cognition, emotion, and motivation. *Psychological Review, 98,* 224–253.

———. (1998). The cultural psychology of personality. *Journal of Cross-Cultural Psychology, 29*(1), 63–87.

Mehrabian, A. (September 1968). Communication without words. *Psychology Today,* 53–55.

Merkin, R. (2006). Uncertainty avoidance: A test of the Hofstede model. *International Journal of Intercultural Relation, 30,* 213–228.

Milstein, T. (2005). Transformation abroad: Sojourning and the perceived enhancement of self-efficacy. *International Journal of Intercultural Relations, 29*(1), 217–238.

Mindess, A. (1999). *Reading between the signs: Intercultural communication for sign language interpreters.* Yarmouth, ME: Intercultural Press.

Molinsky, A., Krabbenhoft, M., Ambady, N., & Choi, Y. (2005). Cracking the non-verbal code: Intercultural competence and gesture recognition across cultures. *Journal of Cross-Cultural Psychology, 36,* 283–303.

Nakano, I. (2006). Silence and politeness in intercultural communication in university seminars. *Journal of Pragmatics, 38,* 1811–1835.

Ng, W., & Roberts, J. (2007). "Helping the family": The mediating role of outside directors in ethnic family firms. *Human Relations, 60,* 285–314.

Noe, R., Hollenbeck, J., Gerhart, B., & Wright, P. (2008). *Human resource management* (6th ed.). New York: McGraw Hill.

Oh, M., Chung, M-H., & Labianca, G. (2004). Group social capital and group effectiveness: The role of informal socializing ties. *Academy of Management Journal, 47,* 893–906.

Osland, J., & Bird, A. (2000). Beyond sophisticated stereotyping: Cultural sensemaking in context. *The Academy of Management Executive, 14*(1), 65–79.

Park, J., Choi, I., & Cho, G. (2006). The actor-observer bias in beliefs of interpersonal insights. *Journal of Cross-Cultural Psychology, 37,* 630–642.

Pollock, D. C., & Van Reken, R. E. (1999). *The third culture kid experience.* Yarmouth, ME: Intercultural Press.

Richardson, R., & Smith, S. (2007). The influence of high/low-context culture and power distance on choice of communication media: Students' media choice to communicate with professors in Japan and America. *International Journal of Intercultural Relations, 31,* 479–501.

Risen, J., Gilovich, T., & Dunning, D. (2007). One-shot illusory correlations and stereotype formation. *Personality and Social Psychology Bulletin, 33,* 1492–1502.

Rogerson-Revell, P. (2007). Humour in business: A double-edged sword. A study of humour and style shifting in intercultural business meetings. *Journal of Pragmatics, 39,* 4–28.

Ross, L. (1977). The intuitive psychologist and his shortcomings. In L. Berkowitz (Ed.), *Advances in experimental social psychology* (vol. 10, pp. 173–220). New York: Academic Press.

Rubenfeld, S., Clement, R., Vibnograd, J., Lussier, D., Amireault, V., Auger, R., & LeBrun, M. (2007). Becoming a cultural intermediary: A further social corollary of second-language learning. *Journal of Language and Social Psychology, 26*, 182–203.

Sanchez-Burks, J., Lee, F., Nisbett, R., & Ybarra, O. (2007). Cultural training based on a theory of relational ideology. *Basic and Applied Social Psychology, 29*, 257–268.

Schouten, B. (2007). Self-construals and conversational indirectness: A Dutch perspective. *International Journal of Intercultural Relation, 31*, 293–297.

Schwartz, S. (2007). Universalism values and the inclusiveness of our moral universe. *Journal of Cross-Cultural Psychology, 38*, 711–728.

Shay, J., & Baack, S. (2004). Expatriate assignment, adjustment, and effectiveness: An empirical examination of the big picture. *Journal of International Business Studies, 35*, 216–232.

Shenkar, O., & Luo, Y. (2008). *International business* (2nd ed.). Thousand Oaks, CA: Sage.

Shigemasu, E., & Ikeda, K. (2006). Face threatening act avoidance and relationship satisfaction between international students and Japanese host students. *International Journal of Intercultural Relations, 30*, 439–455.

Shute, E. (2007). Clashing cultures: A model of international student conflict. *Journal of Cross-Cultural Psychology, 38*, 750–771.

Simpson, J. (2007). Psychological foundations of trust. *Current Directions in Psychological Science, 16*, 264–268.

Singelis, T. (Ed.). (1998). *Teaching about culture, ethnicity, and diversity. Exercises and planned activities.* Thousand Oaks, CA: Sage.

Smith, P., & Schwartz, S. (1997). Values. In J. Berry, M. Segall, & C. Kagitcibasi (Eds.), *Handbook of cross-cultural psychology, vol. 3: Behavior and applications* (2nd ed., pp. 77–118). Boston, MA: Allyn and Bacon.

Stewart, W., & Roth, P. (2001). Risk propensity differences between entrepreneurs and managers: A meta-analytic review. *Journal of Applied Psychology, 86*, 145–153.

Steyn, M., & Grant, T. (2007). "A real bag of mixed emotions": Re-entry experiences of South African exiles. *International Journal of Intercultural Relation, 31*, 363–389.

Sussman, N. M. (2002). Sojourners to another country: The psychological rollercoaster of cultural transitions. In W. J. Lonner, D. L. Dinnel, S. A. Hayes, & D. N. Sattler (Eds.), *Online readings in psychology and culture* (unit 8, chapter 1) (http://www.wwu.edu/~culture), Center for Cross-Cultural Research, Western Washington University, Bellingham, Washington, U.S.A.

Takeuchi, R., Lepak, D., Marinova, S., & Yun, S. (2007). Nonlinear influences of stressors on general adjustment: The case of Japanese expatriates and their spouses. *Journal of International Business Studies, 38*, 944–960.

Thomas, D., & Inkson, K. (2004). *Cultural intelligence.* San Francisco, CA: Berrett-Koehler Publishers.

Ting-Toomey, S. (1985). Toward a theory of conflict and culture. In W. Gudykunst, L. Stewart, & S. Ting-Toomey (Eds.), *Communication, culture and organizational processes.* Beverly Hills, CA: Sage.

Toyokawa, N. (2006). The functional of the social network formed by Japanese sojourners' wives in the United States. *International Journal of Intercultural Relation, 30,* 185–193.

Triandis, H. (1995). *Individualism & collectivism.* Boulder, CO: Westview.

Uskul, A., Hynie, M., & Lalonde, R. (2004). Interdependence as a mediator between culture and interpersonal closeness for Euro-Canadians and Turks. *Journal of Cross-Cultural Psychology, 35,* 174–191.

Van De Vliert, E. (2007). Climatoeconomic roots of survival versus self-expression cultures. *Journal of Cross-Cultural Psychology, 38,* 156–172.

Vidal, M., Valle, R., Aragon, M., & Brewster, C. (2007). Repatriation adjustment process of business employees: Evidence from Spanish workers. *International Journal of Intercultural Relations, 31,* 317–337.

Wan, C., Chiu, C., Peng, S., & Tam, K. (2007). Measuring cultures through intersubjective cultural norms: Implications for predicting relative identification with two or more cultures. *Journal of Cross-Cultural Psychology, 38,* 213–226.

Wang, M., Brislin, R., Wang, W.-Z., Williams, D., & Chao, J. (2000). *Turning bricks into jade: Critical incidents for mutual understanding among Chinese and Americans.* Yarmouth, ME: Intercultural Press.

Wilkins, R., & Gareis, E. (2007). Emotion expression and the locution "I love you": A cross-cultural study. *International Journal of Intercultural Relation, 30,* 51–75.

Yoo, S., Matsumoto, D., LeRoux, J., & Liu, S. (2006). The influence of emotion recognition and emotion regulation on intercultural adjustment. *International Journal of Intercultural Relations, 30,* 345–363.

Yoshida, T. (1994). Interpersonal versus non-interpersonal realities: An effective tool individualists can use to better understand collectivists. In R. Brislin & T. Yoshida (Eds.), *Improving intercultural interactions: Modules for cross-cultural training programs* (p. 243). Thousand Oaks, CA: Sage.

Zimbardo, P., & Leippe, M. (1991). *The psychology of attitude change and social influence.* New York: McGraw-Hill.

Index

About the Author

RICHARD BRISLIN is a Shidler College Distinguished Professor and Professor of Management at the Shidler College of Business, University of Hawaii. He has been awarded the University of Hawaii Regents' Medal for excellence in teaching and is frequently asked to give workshops for American and Asian managers working on international assignments. He is codeveloper of materials used in cross-cultural training programs and is author of a text in cross-cultural psychology. Brislin's PhD in psychology is from Pennsylvania State University.